P9-APJ-181

NORDEN

Crossroads of Destiny

NORDEN

Crossroads of Destiny

by Vincent H. Malmström

Associate Professor of Geography
Middlebury College

A SEARCHLIGHT ORIGINAL

D. VAN NOSTRAND COMPANY, INC.

PRINCETON, NEW JERSEY

TORONTO   LONDON

NEW YORK

Preface

THE five states of Northern Europe—the three Scandinavian countries together with Finland and Iceland—constitute a well-defined regional subdivision of the European subcontinent. This region, which the Scandinavians call "Norden" (literally, "the North"), owes its identity not so much to the facts of physical geography as to the bonds of history and culture which link these northern lands and peoples. In all five states, people of a common ethnic and linguistic background are to be found, though only as a minority in one of the countries. In all five states the overwhelming majority of the population profess the same religious faith. With the exception of Denmark, each of the countries has, at some time in its history, come under the political control of one or another of its northern neighbors. (With the exception of Sweden, all of the countries have also been politically dominated by non-Nordic countries for longer or shorter periods.) In each of the countries the population is small and the resource base niggardly and unbalanced. Yet, despite the marginal quality of the lands they inhabit, all five northern peoples enjoy a standard of living which ranks among the highest in Europe. Moreover, the standards of health, education, and welfare in Norden are among the highest in the world. The Nordic peoples share common economic and social outlooks, and they are fortified by an active desire to preserve and promote their regional identity. Indeed, the nations of Norden are united in all but a political sense.

It is the purpose of this volume to explore the differences in political outlook of the five Nordic states and the facts of geography and history which lie behind them. Why, we may ask, if these states have so much in common with one another, have they never achieved a community of political outlook or interest? What role does each of the Nordic states play in current world affairs? What importance do they have in the global strategy of the "Cold War" or the "peaceful coexistence" which dominates the international scene today? What prospects does the future hold for them? In seeking to answer these questions, we shall first look at Norden as a region, in terms of its physical setting and its cultural heritage. Next, we shall examine each of the countries individually and, finally, attempt to assess the changing strategic significance of Norden as a whole.

As a by-product of several years of residence, research, and travel in Norden, this volume undoubtedly reflects the bias of one who is more than sympathetic with the problems of these small countries and more than a little impressed with their accomplishments. Within these limitations the author has striven to be as objective as possible, and he willingly assumes the responsibility for any errors of interpretation. He has purposely presented his material with a strong historical slant, first, because he is firmly convinced that an understanding of the contemporary scene is impossible without an appreciation of the political evolution of the Nordic states, and second, because some aspects of this history are not generally known outside of the Scandinavian region.

For the mechanical preparation of this manuscript he is indebted to Jennifer Nelson, Edith Harrison, and Susan Hanson. For their reluctant cooperation in providing the necessary "peace and quiet" for its writing, he can only thank his family.

VINCENT H. MALMSTRÖM

Middlebury, Vermont

Contents

Maps (following p. 64)

1   *Norden: The Physical Setting*

LYING as it does on the very northern margins of Europe, Norden has always enjoyed a certain degree of detachment from the rest of the continent. In this respect it resembles the British Isles, but unlike the United Kingdom, the states of Norden have seldom had either the cause or the means to involve themselves in the political affairs of their continental neighbors. When they have become involved, it has almost invariably been to their detriment.

This detachment may be ascribed to the configuration of the region, for as the map reveals, Norden is composed of peninsulas and islands. The largest continuous land mass is the Fenno-Scandian peninsula. This compound neck of land is joined to the subcontinent between the Gulf of Finland and the White Sea. Despite the relative breadth of the peninsula's base, few peoples have moved across this bridge during the course of history. Ancient crystalline hills covered by dense stands of spruce and pine and dotted by thousands of lakes and swamps discouraged its use as a major access route into Norden.

From its base, the Fenno-Scandian peninsula broadens into a lobe between the Gulfs of Finland and Bothnia—an area which comprises the core of the present Finnish state. To the north the peninsula contracts into an isthmus scarcely 200 miles across, measured between the inner ends of the Gulfs of Bothnia and Kandalaksha. Thereafter it broadens again into (1) the Kola peninsula, which reaches 300 miles to the east and lies entirely within the Soviet Union, and (2) the Scandinavian peninsula, which extends 1200 miles to the southwest. The latter may be said to consist of two rather distinct lobes as well, which have become the core areas of the states of Norway and Sweden, respectively. The fact that the irregular Fenno-Scandian peninsula embraces three sovereign states and a salient of a fourth does not detract from its physical unity; instead it serves to emphasize that historical and cultural factors have contributed more to the political diversity of the region than have physical ones.

Norden has one other land tie with Europe, and that is the peninsula of Jutland. Although this is little more than 40 miles wide at its base, its lowland character and strategic location have made it a much more important land approach to Norden than the broader but less accessible Fenno-Scandian peninsula. Jutland constitutes almost two-thirds of the area of the Danish homeland, but it is not the core area of the Danish realm.

With the exception of these two peninsulas, the land areas within Norden are islands. East of Jutland lie the Danish home islands, over 400 in number, but only 100 of which are inhabited. Despite the fact that their combined area is only half that of Jutland, the Danish archipelago is the real economic nerve center—and hence the political core—of the Danish state. Together with Jutland, the Danish home islands control the southern land approaches to the Scandinavian peninsula, for the straits which separate them are nowhere wider than 10 miles and in most places much less. For the same reason, the Danish archipelago also controls the sea approaches to the Baltic—a fact which allowed the Danes to exact a toll from each vessel passing into or out of the Baltic until as recently as 1857.

Among the other Baltic islands belonging to Norden are the Swedish islands of Gotland and Öland and the Finnish Åland archipelago. Of the two Swedish islands, Gotland is strategically situated near the middle of the Baltic and serves as something of an advance outpost in that country's defense system. The Finnish-controlled Åland islands likewise occupy a strategic position, for they span the entrance to the Gulf of Bothnia, the Baltic's northern extremity.

The boundaries of Norden reach far out into the Atlantic and Arctic Oceans, embracing there the Faeroes, Iceland, Svalbard (Spitsbergen), and Greenland. The latter, while physically a part of

North America, is politically an administrative county of Denmark —a county over 50 times larger than the rest of the country! The Faeroes are also a county of Denmark, but have considerable local autonomy. Iceland, a Danish territory until 1944, is once again an independent republic. Svalbard was awarded to Norwegian jurisdiction by the League of Nations with the proviso that any prior claimants to the islands still active in mining coal there be allowed to continue such activity. The only state which exercises this privilege is the Soviet Union.

Thus far, we have examined Norden's location and configuration only with respect to the more conventional land and sea approaches. But here, as everywhere, the Air Age has opened an entirely new dimension as regards location. Moreover, it has immensely broadened the horizons of interaction. Today, contacts between Norden on the one hand and North America and Asia on the other are both frequent and commonplace. Indeed, if anything, the Air Age has pushed Norden closer to the middle of the world arena, and thereby increased its strategic importance many-fold.

To appreciate this fact, one must put away the flat maps and look at a globe. Take a string and stretch it between the two major political centers of the modern world, Washington and Moscow. The line thus traced represents the shortest distance between these two centers, the so-called "Great Circle" route. Map 1 will afford a fair approximation of the globe for this purpose. This route, after it leaves the coast of North America, passes over the southern tip of Greenland, Iceland, central Norway and Sweden, and the Finnish capital of Helsinki before entering the territory of the Soviet Union. Thus, far from being offside, the Nordic nations today lie squarely between the two major contenders in the East-West struggle.

Such a location is hardly an enviable one as long as tense relations exist between the two great powers. For this reason, the Nordic countries have assumed a special importance in the defense perimeter which the West has thrown up around itself. Denmark, Norway, and Iceland are all members of the North Atlantic Treaty

Organization and as such have bases and/or forces which contribute to that defensive alliance. On the other hand, Sweden, having been fortunate in avoiding involvement in two previous wars, is hoping that her armed neutrality will spare her from an eventual third conflict. At the same time, she is seeking to avoid a Soviet counter-move against Finland, which, as a "good neighbor" to the Soviet Union, has little choice but to be neutral.

Rather than bemoaning the negative aspects of their Air Age location, however, the Scandinavians have sought to exploit its positive aspects. It was they who initiated commercial air transport "over the Pole" to Los Angeles in 1954 and to Tokyo two years later—a pioneering venture at first discounted but now emulated by several competitors.

Latitudinally, Norden is closely akin to Alaska, another region whose location has been enhanced by the Air Age. The southern borders of Denmark lie on the 55th parallel as does the southern extremity of the Alaskan Panhandle. Norway's North Cape, at 71° N., is in the same latitude as Point Barrow. Longitudinally, there is a similar correspondence, for it is as far from the eastern frontier of Finland to the westernmost promontory of Iceland as it is from the Alaskan Panhandle to the outermost Aleutian Islands. In terms of size, however, Alaska's massive mainland block gives her one-eighth more area than all the peninsulas and islands of Norden put together (less, of course, Greenland, which by itself is more than half again as large as Alaska). But the real difference in size between our 49th state and Norden is in the size of their respective populations. Whereas Alaska can boast of scarcely one-quarter million inhabitants, the Nordic countries have a combined population of some 20 millions.

A MARGINAL RESOURCE BASE

With an area which comprises one-sixth of all of Europe west of the Soviet Union, the Nordic countries nevertheless have only one-twentieth of Europe's total population. Here is eloquent testimony to the marginal quality of these northern lands. This may be further demonstrated by citing a few statistics as to land use within the region. Only 10 percent is in agricultural production (of which 8 percent is cultivated and 2 percent natural meadows), some 45 percent is classified as forest, and a like percentage is described as "other land"—that is, bare rock, swamp, sand, etc. In effect, therefore, it may be said that the Nordic peoples are living off only half their land; the other half is essentially an economic millstone around their necks.

Many factors contribute to the marginal nature of the Northern countries. To be sure, their high northerly latitude may be considered something of a handicap in itself. Nevertheless, the effects of latitude are in part offset by an inordinately mild climate, for the prevailing air flow over the entire region at all seasons is from the southwest off the Atlantic. As a result, winter temperatures in the Lofoten islands of Norway, for example, range more than 40° F. above the average for their latitude. On the other hand, altitude has a negative effect, lowering the temperature some 3.5° F. for every 1000-foot rise. As a consequence, in rugged countries such as Norway and Iceland, considerable areas lie above both the upper limit of cultivation and the tree line.

Terrain makes its effects felt in several other ways as well. For example, in many parts of Norway and Iceland the sheer ruggedness of relief restricts man's places of settlement and utilization of the land. Where major topographic barriers rise in the path of the prevailing moisture-laden winds, as in both Norway and Iceland, there is an extremely heavy concentration of precipitation on the windward slope. Because of latitude and elevation, much of this moisture falls in the form of snow, not only nourishing the largest icefields in Europe but also severely complicating all overland communications during the winter. The same topographic barriers have a marked "weather divide" effect, separating the more maritime windward slopes from the more continental leeward slopes. Thus, in the Fenno-Scandian states there are stronger contrasts in climate from west to east than there are from north to south.

Geologically the five Northern countries show great variety but, apart from Sweden, little wealth. The Fenno-Scandian countries consist chiefly of ancient crystalline rock which is locally rich in iron ore, copper, and certain other metals. Such a crystalline structure, however, precludes the presence of fossil fuels; hence, the lack of coal and petroleum is sorely felt. Iceland, which is entirely volcanic in origin, has no mineral deposits of commercial importance today, though some sulfur and Iceland spar (calcite) were mined in the past. Denmark, which is almost exclusively underlain by limestone and chalk, is the one Nordic country where at least the structure would seem to permit the occurrence of oil. However, all drilling to date has produced only dry wells.

The deficiency in fossil fuels is fortunately compensated in part by the presence—in at least the more rugged parts of Norden—of bountiful supplies of water power. Here Norway, Sweden, and Iceland are decidedly well off, Finland only moderately so, and Denmark without any potential of importance.

The existence of great water-power reserves in the higher areas of Norden stems in large measure from the fact that repeated glaciation has steepened the valleys and impounded the streams in a series of lakes. The same ice sheets, however, were responsible for removing most of the soil cover from the Fenno-Scandian countries and depositing much of it in Denmark and the adjacent areas of Germany and Poland. What remains in the Fenno-Scandian countries is largely sand, gravel, and boulders either strewn helter-skelter by the ice itself or washed out of the ice by melt-water streams. To be sure, Denmark has much infertile sand and gravel as well, but where the glaciers ground their way over the limestone and chalk they produced what are the most productive soils in Norden today. In Iceland the story was much the same as in the Fenno-Scandian states, though there fine dust (loess) blown off the front of the melting ice accumulated in lowland pockets, providing the best soils that that country possesses. Unfortunately, the destruction of most of the original birch forests in Iceland has exposed many of these loess deposits to frightful wind erosion, and in several areas of the island the deserts of sand and gravel are advancing.

But if the glacier was unkind to the Fenno-Scandian states in terms of soil, the after effects of the ice proved more beneficial. While the great glaciers lay over the land, they depressed the surface with their massive weight. Then as they began to melt, the sea level rose, flooding many of the lower valleys. There thick beds of marine clay were deposited, only to be exposed as the land itself emerged after being freed from its burden of ice. Today the clay soils of Norway, Sweden, and Finland rank among the best that these states possess.

Perhaps the best indicator of the combined effects of terrain, climate, and soil is to be found in the native vegetation. In most of Denmark and the adjacent areas of southwestern Sweden this consisted chiefly of beech and oak. Over most of southern Sweden and along the southwest coasts of Norway and Finland the forest was mixed, containing both the aforementioned broadleaf trees and considerable spruce and pine. Most of the remaining area of the Fenno-Scandian countries belongs to the belt of dense coniferous stands known as the taiga. Only in the far north and in the higher mountain areas of Norway and Sweden do we find widespread areas of scrub birch. Above these in turn are the broad open expanses of the *fjell,* or *viddas,* clothed only in hardy dwarf species of birch, mountain ash, and willow, together with heather, crowberries, and juniper. Much of lowland Iceland was once covered by scrub birch forests as well, but man and his livestock have been responsible for a large share of the barren nakedness we find there today. That trees can and do grow successfully in Iceland has been demonstrated by numerous experimental plantations.

There can be little doubt but that the marginal qualities of Norden's physical environment have militated against the emergence of a political power of any great consequence within the region. Small-power status is a fact of life that the Nordic states have learned to live with during the past two hundred years. It is precisely this "smallness," this "weakness," in combination with their growing strategic importance that poses the most difficult problem for them individually and as a group in current world affairs. Must they align themselves with some great power or power bloc to further their own best interests? Or can a small state better preserve its political identity as a neutral? This is a question which not only divides the nations of Norden, but also troubles many a small country in every corner of the globe today.

THE GEOPOLITICAL SIGNIFICANCE OF THE PHYSICAL SETTING

Besides contributing to the marginal nature of Norden's resource base, each aspect of the region's physical setting has a distinct geopolitical significance of its own. For a moment let us consider some of the more specific implications of Norden's location. The fact that Denmark controls the straits between the North and Baltic Seas means that all oceangoing ships using the ports of East Germany, Poland, the Baltic Soviet Republics, and Leningrad must pass through Danish waters. In addition, Norway flanks the only ice-free entrance into the Arctic Ocean through more than 1000 miles of its sheltered, deep-water fjord coast. Every vessel moving in and out of Murmansk, the only Soviet port with year-round access to the open Atlantic, can easily be kept under surveillance from bases in Norway or Iceland. Thus, Soviet access to the major shipping lanes of the North Atlantic is contingent upon traversing ocean "narrows" controlled by the three Nordic states aligned with NATO.

The political significance of Norden's climatic patterns can largely be demonstrated by the events of history, though even today they are not without their importance. For example, the success of many a military campaign was dependent on the severity of a given winter. A cold winter meant firm ice, a fact which greatly altered the strategic significance of many fortified points located on lakes or waterways. Winter was also the season of greatest overland mobility, for then heavy goods could easily be transported by sled, and the use of skis facilitated movement over stumps and stones and lakes and swamps in a way that no other vehicle at any other season could effect. Winter was the season when the great commercial fairs were held and when the bishops made their *visitas* to all the churches in their respective dioceses. Indeed, many an ecclesiastical and political boundary in medieval Scandinavia was drawn in terms of a region's accessibility in winter. Thus, the east Norwegian valleys of Valdres and Hallingdal belonged to the bishopric of Stavanger on the southwest coast, while the presently Swedish territory of Jämtland in central Scandinavia lay historically within the Norwegian sphere of influence.

To be sure, it was not climate alone which influenced such patterns of orientation. Topography, too, has contributed mightily to regional differentiation, especially in Norway. There a long history of local isolation manifests itself in a variety of linguistic dialects unparalleled in the other Northern countries. There internal political differences demonstrate stronger patterns of regional concentration than elsewhere in Norden. And there the boundaries of the political subdivisions reproduce more faithfully the major lineaments of the terrain than they do in any other Nordic state, with the possible exception of Iceland.

Of fully as great importance as a factor in fixing boundaries within Norden has been the vegetation. In Norway and Sweden, especially, one finds many illustrations of the divisive effects that the dark stands of coniferous forest had on the economic, social, and political patterns of earlier days. Sections of provincial and national boundaries alike can be found which owe their alignments to broad belts of inhospitable and sparsely populated woodland. In Sweden of the Middle Ages geographic orientation was frequently expressed in such terms as *nordanskog* and *sunnanskog* (that is, "north of the forest" and "south of the forest"), much in the same way that Norwegians spoke of *nordenfjellske* and *söndenfjellske* Norway (that is, "Norway north of the mountains" and "Norway south of the mountains"). So real was the obstacle posed by the forest that wherever an alternate route presented itself, it was chosen regardless of the distance. The old Norwegian proverb *Skogene skiller, viddene binder sammen* ("The forests divide, the mountain plateaus unite") provides insight into why some of the medieval patterns of orientation took the form they did, as, for example, the westward connection of Valdres and Hallingdal to Stavanger.

There are perhaps few areas in the world where soil patterns have reflected themselves so strongly in the state-making process as they have in Norden. Certainly, the viability of any state is in large part determined by the success and stability of its agriculture; these, in turn, are conditioned by the relative productivity of its soils. Thus, in all five of the Northern countries the major and most enduring center of political power has developed in that region possessing the best soils. Each of these favored regions became the core, or political heartland, of its respective country. In Norway it was the easily weathered Cambro-Silurian deposits of the lower eastern valleys and the marine clays of the Oslofjord region that nurtured the first local kingdoms. In Sweden it was the marine clays of the Central Lowland that gave sustenance to both the Swedish and Gothic nations. In Finland the center of economic and political power has always lain in the clay plains of the southern and western coastal districts. In Denmark, although each major component of the realm—be it peninsula or island—initially gave rise to its own political center, all of these lay on the lime-rich ground moraine of the east; none of them was found in the sterile outwash sands of western Jutland. Even in Iceland, a state which never developed a truly agricultural (that is, crop-producing) economy, the focus of political power has always been the Southern Lowlands, a region whose productivity is unequaled elsewhere on the island.

In only one of the Northern countries has the presence of mineral deposits played a significant role in the political evolution of the state. This country is Sweden, which during the Middle Ages ranked as a major exporter of both copper and iron. The revenues earned by their export, as well as the armaments they helped to produce, accounted for much of the prowess Sweden enjoyed as a "Great Power" before 1700. However, as we have noted above, the absence of first-rate coal deposits and of petroleum may be advanced as a partial explanation for the lower-class power status which the Northern countries have been obliged to assume since the dawn of the Industrial Revolution. Lack of the necessary raw materials prevented the Northern countries from industrializing either as early or as rapidly as their better-endowed neighbors to the south. Yet, the relative lateness of the coming of industry to Scandinavia has had geopolitical consequences which, on sum, have probably been more beneficial than detrimental.

For one thing, the tardy industrialization of Norden encouraged a proportionately greater tide of overseas migration to take place from this region than from any other major subdivision of Europe. A steadily growing labor force on the farms found little or no opportunity for employment in the towns. Though viewed as a calamitous loss to the home countries, especially as it swelled to its peak in the 1880's, this outflow of farm sons and daughters served as a "safety valve" at a critical juncture in Norden's economic evolution. Had not these countries been "freed" of these mounting population pressures, it is highly unlikely that they could have raised their living standards as far or as fast as they subsequently did.

Because industrialization in Scandinavia was largely dependent upon and coincident with the harnessing of electrical energy, the geographic distribution of industry was far more dispersed than in Britain or Germany, where most industrial activity was localized in the coal fields. Instead of creating giant urban centers filled with endless rows of factories and dwellings, industry invaded the Scandinavian landscape in a much more subtle way. The clean "white coal" of hydroelectricity precluded the blight of "Black Countries," smog, and workers' slums from developing, for as often as not, factories grew up amidst the idyllic rural settings of lakes and forests. Never did the problems of congestion, housing, and sanitation even remotely approach the dimensions of those in the Midlands or the Ruhr. And never did the economic, social, and political gaps between classes widen into the abysmal gulfs which characterized so many other industrializing nations of Europe. Surely, much of the stability and homogeneity which the Northern countries demonstrate today is a consequence of the unobtrusive manner in which they made their conversion from rural-agricultural societies to urban-industrial states.

2 *Norden: The Cultural Heritage*

D~ESPITE~ their physical diversity, the countries of Norden demonstrate strong cultural homogeneity within and among themselves. Only two major ethnic groups are represented within the region, namely the "Germanics," who are principally of the "Nordic" physical type, and the "Finno-Ugrians," who belong to the "East Baltic" type. Where the two have come into contact with each other, as in Finland and Lappland, fusion has been going on for centuries. Elsewhere on the Nordic periphery intermixture with other physical types has occurred in the past. For example, in Iceland a considerable Celtic infusion took place, and in Greenland the present populace is descended from mixed Nordic-Eskimo stock.

THE LANGUAGES OF NORDEN

In all five of the Northern countries, languages are spoken which derive from a common Germanic origin. During Viking times the tongue known as Old Norse evolved into an East Norse, spoken in Sweden and Denmark, and a West Norse, spoken in Norway, the Faeroes, and Iceland. In the Middle Ages the three Scandinavian languages became further differentiated. In Sweden the strong Hanseatic influence on commerce, mining, and town administration is reflected in the many German words which entered the Swedish language at the time. In Norway the medieval domination of the country's economic and political life by the Danes resulted in a linguistic schism which has perpetuated itself to the present. In the southern and eastern districts of Norway a Dano-

Norwegian language developed which contrasted markedly with the old West Norse dialects which continued to be spoken in the more isolated valley and fjord districts. The former came to be known as *riksmål,* or "the national language," while the latter was called *landsmål,* or "the rural language." Both terms carried inaccurate connotations, however, for neither was the one a "national" language nor was the other exclusively used in the rural districts, particularly after large-scale migration began to the towns. The present official designations of the two languages are equally misleading, for *riksmål* is now known as *bokmål* ("the literary language"), though there is an extensive literature in the other as well, and *landsmål* is now *nynorsk* ("new Norwegian"), although it represents the systematization of essentially medieval dialects. At the present time, a gradual enforced fusion of the two languages is being carried out in an effort to produce a new tongue known as *samnorsk* ("common Norwegian"). Because it is a language native to no one, its opponents derisively refer to it as *skamnorsk,* or "shameful Norwegian."

The Swedish conquest and colonization of Finland during the Middle Ages led to an enduring bilingualism in that country as well. The Finnish language is closely related to Estonian and distantly allied with Hungarian, but has no familial tie with either of its Indo-European neighbors, Swedish or Russian. It has, however, incorporated many Swedish terms into its vocabulary, especially those having to do with the more advanced technology and with social and political institutions introduced from the west. Nevertheless, at the beginning of the nineteenth century, nearly one-fifth of the population of Finland spoke Swedish as their native language. Today the proportion of Swedish-speaking Finns is only 8 percent, due to their higher degree of urbanization and consequently lower rate of natural increase and to their greater tendency to emigrate during the latter part of the last century. Geographically, the Swedish-speaking minority in Finland continues to be concentrated along the south and west coasts, so that the knowledge and use of their language falls off sharply toward the northern and eastern interior. Nonetheless, Swedish is accorded the status of an official language of the country, and its value is undiminished as a vehicle of Finnish cultural communication with the rest of Norden.

The present linguistic patterns is Iceland and the Faeroes reflect the geographic isolation of these North Atlantic isles. Modern Icelandic is basically the Norse tongue of its first Viking settlers, so little altered with the passage of time that the sagas of the thirteenth century can still be read in their original form without difficulty. To be sure, the expansion of geographic and scientific horizons which has taken place since that time has necessitated an extensive updating of the vocabulary. In order to preserve the purity of the language, this updating has been done through the conscious creation of new words rather than through the adoption of foreign terms. The language of the Faeroes represents a slightly more evolved form of Norse and apparently traces its origin to a medieval resettlement of the islands from western Norway following their depopulation by the Black Death.

Apart from Finland, none of the Northern countries has a linguistic minority which exceeds 1 percent of the total national population. Denmark has a small number of ethnic Germans in Slesvig, and there are approximately 30,000 Danish-speaking people in German Schleswig. A roughly similar number of Lapps are distributed through the northern areas of Norway, Sweden, and Finland, with about two-thirds of the total residing in Norway. Small groups of ethnic Finns moved into the forest districts of south-central Sweden and Norway during the seventeenth century, and to this day their descendants retain a certain cultural individuality within their so-called *finnskogar* ("Finnish woods"). While linguistic minorities have never constituted a threat to political stability or national unity in any of the Northern countries, it should be pointed out that difference in language is in large part responsible for the semi-autonomy which the Faeroes enjoy within the political framework of Denmark and which the Åland Islands enjoy within the Finnish Republic.

Despite the complete freedom of worship which exists within

the Northern countries, the populace of all five nations belongs over-whelmingly to the Evangelical Lutheran church. In Sweden (which included Finland at the time), the Reformation served both to further the development of Swedish nationalism and to strengthen royal authority. In Denmark and its dominions (which then included Norway, the Faeroes, Iceland, and Greenland), the Reformation provided a vehicle for extending the absolutism of the monarchy. Thus, throughout the North, the "conversion" to Lutheranism was initially a matter of political and economic expedience, rather than any basic "reform" of the public's religious outlook. Nevertheless, once established, Evangelical Lutheranism has remained the state church in each of the countries, and in none of them has more than 5 percent of the populace seen fit to disassociate themselves from it.

ECONOMIC BASES OF NORDIC CULTURE

As has been intimated above, the present ethnic, linguistic, and religious patterns of Norden were developed largely as a consequence of the region's economic evolution. Early Lapp inhabitants of what today is southern Finland were driven progressively northward by tribes of Finnish hunters. When they began moving southward again through the Scandinavian Peninsula, their advance was countered by northward-moving Germanic hunters. Thus pushed into the northernmost reaches of Fenno-Scandia, the Lapps became the heirs of vast areas beyond the tree line where herding reindeer came to provide the entire key to their existence. Though greatly modified, this form of nomadism persists to this day, due to the fact that no other more advanced type of land-use has been able to supplant it. Lappland is beyond the practical limits of agriculture and forestry, and only where mineral deposits occur have local pockets of commercially-oriented economic activity arisen (as in the iron-mining centers of Kiruna, Gällivare, and Kirkenes, seen in Map 4).

While the Lapp and his reindeer-based economy continue to hold sway over the interior and more continental areas of the North, along the Atlantic coast Scandinavian hunters, fishers, and gatherers began to develop a strongly marine-oriented economy. Stocks of larger mammals, such as wild reindeer, elk (the North American moose), bear, wolf, seal, walrus, and polar bear, were decimated rather early, but the vast schools of fish which frequent the waters off western and northern Norway came to constitute a reasonably dependable and secure economic base. Thus, in these marginal coastal regions, fishing continues to form the cornerstone of economy; here, too, more advanced forms of livelihood have not been able to penetrate.

The innovation of farming and stock raising probably reached Norden from the southeast about 2000 B.C. However, it supplanted the earlier hunting and fishing economies very slowly and only in those regions of favorable terrain, soil, and climate. This meant that most of Denmark, apart from the Heath of Jutland, was cleared and that toeholds were established in the lower valleys of the East Country, Tröndelag, and the Jaeren district south of Stavanger in Norway, in Skåne and the central lowlands of Svealand in Sweden, and along the south and west coasts of Finland. In none of the areas, however, did the level of technology or the productivity of the land permit the development of anything more than a subsistence type of farming. As a result, the settlement pattern was dispersed, and agglomerated villages did not develop except in Denmark, where more limited access to ground water (in the form of wells and springs) was a contributing factor. As population densities increased, new lands had to be carved from the reserve of more marginal wilderness which surrounded the existing settlements. Obviously, such internal colonization could only meet with increasingly indifferent success, and by the late eighth century many areas of Scandinavia had seemingly reached their saturation point in terms of population. This no doubt was reflected in the vigorous overseas expansion of the following three centuries—a period which has been termed the Viking Age.

The new horizons which opened for the Scandinavian peoples during the Viking Age resulted in the introduction of commercialism as well as Christianity. Both served as town-building forces, and many central places that lent themselves to the development of trade often had their importance reinforced by religion. This was especially true in Norway, where embryonic towns such as Trondheim (first called Nidaros), Stavanger, Hamar, and Oslo had both a religious and commercial basis. Usually, however, the locational requirements of commerce were quite different from those of religion, and where towns grew up around ancient Viking centers of worship, as in Ribe, Viborg, and Roskilde in Denmark, and in Lund, Skara, and Uppsala in Sweden, they were generally overshadowed by the end of the Middle Ages by more strategically located commercial towns, such as Aarhus, Copenhagen, Malmö, and Stockholm. A similar fate was suffered by most of the ancient *ting,* or assembly sites, some of which were abandoned altogether (as at Frosta and Gulen in Norway), while others (such as those near Aabenraa and Ringsted in Denmark) gave rise to towns of relatively modest size.

Commercially, Norden quickly passed into the sphere of the Hanseatic League, which soon developed a flourishing exchange of fish, timber, and furs for such staples as bread grains and salt. While Bergen became the great emporium of the North Atlantic fish trade, Visby became the focal point of Baltic commerce. About the same time, largely under Hanseatic direction, the mines of the Bergslagen district of central Sweden began operation, with copper coming from Falun and iron from around Grängesberg.

With the passing of the Hansa, Dutch merchants gradually assumed control over a major segment of Nordic commerce, and a great upswing in timber trade, especially with the Norwegian South Country, took place. By the time that British commercial interests had begun turning their attention toward Norden, the domestic economies of Denmark and Sweden had transformed these countries into viable nation-states, with the latter gradually surpassing the former thanks to its superior resource endowment. Though Norwegian silver mines at Kongsberg and copper mines in the Dovre Mountains poured considerable treasures into the coffers of

Denmark, they could not match the wealth of the Bergslagen, which, by the end of the Middle Ages, had assured Sweden's status as the greatest economic and political power in Northern Europe.

THE COMING OF INDUSTRY

The expansion of commercial agriculture, forestry, fishing, and mining was restricted largely to the core areas of Denmark, Sweden, Norway, and Finland, while subsistence forms of livelihood persisted in Iceland and the northern parts of Fenno-Scandia. When the technological innovations of industrialization reached Norden in the early nineteenth century, most of the early development took place near water-power sites, such as at Sarpsborg in Norway, around Göteborg in Sweden, and at Tampere in Finland. On the other hand, steam-powered industries were dependent on imported coal, so port cities such as Oslo, Copenhagen, Stockholm, and Helsinki also developed concentrations of factories. The subsequent development of hydroelectric power in Norway, Sweden, Finland, and Iceland has given industrial impetus to scores of other towns, among them Reykjavík. In Norway the largest water-power resources are located on the edges of the Hardanger Plateau close to the centers of population. In Sweden, on the other hand, the primary sources of hydroelectricity are situated in Norrland, far to the north of the main population clusters. Consequently, some of the world's longest high tension transmission lines have had to be constructed to deliver this power to where it is needed.

With industrialization came improved transportation, first in the form of railways and then as automobile highways. The former developed a relatively dense network in Denmark and the core areas of Norway, Sweden, and Finland, but only widely spaced tentacles in the northern areas of Fenno-Scandia. In Iceland and the most remote parts of Lappland, the railway age has been bypassed altogether, so that highways and airplanes provide the only forms of modern transportation, apart from coastwise steamers.

In the wake of industrial growth and improved communications, the population of Norden has not only expanded dramatically in numbers, but it has also contracted in its areal distribution. Thus, while densities have increased in the more favored areas as urbanization accelerated, many outlying rural areas, particularly those of marginal economies, have suffered marked declines. From a total of 5 million at the beginning of the nineteenth century, the population of Norden had grown to 20 million by 1960. As Table 1 shows, the present density of population per square mile of gross area

Table 1   *Comparison of Population Densities in Norden and in Anglo-America, 1961*

COUNTRY	POPULATION IN 000's	DENSITY PER SQUARE MILE OF	
		GROSS AREA	CULTIVABLE AREA
DENMARK	4,617	275	427
FINLAND	4,467	34	395
ICELAND	180	5	8,620
NORWAY	3,611	28	1,025
SWEDEN	7,542	44	495
NORDEN	20,417	91	625
UNITED STATES	183,650	50	250
CANADA	18,269	5	115

(*Source:* Compiled from United Nations, *Demographic Yearbook,* and statistical publications of the individual countries.)

is less in all the Nordic countries, apart from Denmark, than it is in the United States, though only Iceland is comparable to Canada. However, when the man/land ratio is expressed in terms of cultivable area, it is everywhere much higher in Norden than in Anglo-America and reaches extreme values in Iceland and Norway.

In Table 2, the vital statistics of population of Norden are compared to those of the United States and Canada. Apart from Iceland, all of the Northern countries have considerably lower birth rates than Anglo-America. On the other hand, Sweden and Denmark have slightly higher death rates than the United States. This is not due to infant mortality, which is substantially lower in all

Table 2 *Comparison of Selected Vital Statistics in Norden and in Anglo-America, 1961*

	RATE PER 1,000				WOMEN PER	LIFE EXPECTANCY		AGE GROUPS (%)		
COUNTRY	BIRTHS	DEATHS	NATURAL INCREASE	INFANT MORTALITY	1,000 MEN	MEN	WOMEN	0-14	15-64	65+
DENMARK	16.6	9.5	7.1	22.5	1,016	66.9	72.6	25.7	63.9	10.4
FINLAND	18.4	9.0	9.4	19.8	1,080	63.4	69.8	30.2	62.6	7.2
ICELAND	27.4	6.6	20.8	13.3	978	66.1	70.3	34.7	57.4	7.9
NORWAY	17.5	9.1	8.4	18.7	1,007	71.1	74.7	25.9	63.2	10.9
SWEDEN	13.9	9.8	4.1	15.5	1,005	70.9	74.4	22.2	66.0	11.8
NORDEN	16.2	9.4	6.8	18.6	1,024	68.3	73.0	25.5	64.2	10.3
UNITED STATES	23.4	9.3	14.1	25.2	1,030	66.5	73.0	31.1	59.7	9.2
CANADA	26.0	7.7	18.3	27.3	973	67.6	72.9	33.5	59.0	7.5

Source: Compiled from United Nations, *Demographic Yearbook,* and statistical publications of the individual countries.

Nordic countries, but to a higher proportion of elderly people. The greatest disproportion in the sexes is found in Finland, where losses of males during World War II were especially heavy. Thus, Norden as a whole demonstrates the characteristics of a mature, economically advanced region, with a rate of natural increase less than half that of Anglo-America. Thanks to the large-scale emigration which took place on the eve of industrialization, population growth has not outrun economic development, as it has in so many parts of the world. On the contrary, the population base was so modest to begin with that the per capita increase in wealth has been the greatest of any region in Europe. As a result the countries of Norden today enjoy a higher material standard of living than any comparable grouping on the subcontinent.

There is little doubt but that the achievement of a relatively affluent society within the limitations of a marginal resource base has been accomplished through the evolution of an increasingly planned economy. As proponents of the "Middle Way," the Nordic countries have been acclaimed for their pioneering strides toward full economic and social democracy. Critics like to point to the high rate of "human attrition" which the welfare state supposedly has engendered, and Sweden, as the most affluent of the Nordic states, is particularly singled out for attack. Such "degeneracy" is difficult to prove, especially when one notes that the suicide rate in "capitalist" West Germany, Switzerland, and Austria is higher than it is in Sweden, that the net alcoholic consumption per capita in the United States is about double what it is in Sweden, and that the American murder rate is seven and a half times greater than Sweden's. Norden's economic prosperity is in large part the product of domestic tranquility, which in turn may be ascribed to the region's small, highly literate, and homogeneous population. That these five countries should have evolved to such a uniformly high level, despite their great diversity in physical endowments, is all the more impressive when we realize that their political evolution as states likewise followed very different paths. It is to the examination of the individual countries that we now turn our attention.

3 _Denmark: Crossroads of the North_

B Y VIRTUE of its strategic location astride the east-west water routes which connect the North and Baltic Seas and the north-south land routes between the continent and the Scandinavian Peninsula, Denmark has very aptly been called the "Crossroads of Northern Europe." The advent of the Air Age has not diminished the significance of Denmark's location but, on the contrary, has only served to further enhance it, as illustrated by the choice of Copenhagen's Kastrup Airport as the main traffic center of the Scandinavian Airlines System. Now, more than at any time in the past, Denmark is truly the "Gateway to Scandinavia."

The origins of the Danish state go back to about the time that the Roman Empire was crumbling. Two separate foci of power had already developed—one in South Jutland, the other on the island of Sjaelland. Both centers were in a position to dominate vital routeways between the North and Baltic Seas, the former to command the land link established by Frisian traders up the Eider river to its headwaters and over a low divide to Slien fjord, and the latter to control the straits of the Öresund and the Great Belt. Because the isthmian route carried the bulk of the commerce, it naturally became the primary target of Danish expansion. Danish Vikings not only followed it west to its destination in Dorstad (present-day Dordrecht), but also beyond into England, Ireland, and France. It was during the Viking period that the first Danish commercial center arose at Hedeby (modern Schleswig) and that earthenwork ramparts (_Dannevirke_) were thrown up to protect the route on its southern landward approaches. However, the Viking conquest and colonization of eastern England (*Danelaw*) and Normandy could not be sustained, and as Danish blood and culture were diluted, Danish political power was eroded. The conversion of the Danes to Christianity likewise had the effect of diverting their energies from the west.

THE STRUGGLE WITH THE GERMANS

The introduction of Christianity to Denmark was itself accompanied by considerable political side-play. Because the original conversion was accomplished from North Germany, the first cathedrals at Schleswig, Ribe, and Aarhus were staffed with German clergy. To counteract the German influence, King Knut ("Canute the Great") brought in English clergy to establish bishoprics at Odense, Roskilde, and Lund. In a further effort to weaken German influence, Roskilde was made the country's capital and in 1104 Lund was proclaimed the archepiscopal see of all Norden.

Danish freedom from German authority depended, of course, on the strength of the South Jutland frontier. At the same time, Danish unity depended on avoiding the creation of a South Jutland realm which would become strong enough to challenge the central government. This political dilemma, compounded with religious issues, invited intrigue, intervention, and disorder, and not until 1157 did Valdemar the Great emerge as sole king of Denmark. But while unity had been achieved, independence had not, for Valdemar owed his throne to the support of the German emperor.

During Valdemar's reign the defenses of the realm were greatly improved. Fortresses were built at Havn (now Copenhagen) to guard the southern entrance to the Öresund and at Nyborg to protect the Great Belt, while the Dannevirke was also strongly reinforced. Shortly after Valdemar's death, the outbreak of civil wars in the German states encouraged the Danes to invade and conquer almost all of Pomerania and Mecklenburg. German counterattacks were not only beaten down, but Valdemar's son ("Valdemar the Victorious") also captured both Lübeck and Hamburg, thereby forcing the German emperor to acknowledge him as his equal. In succeeding decades, Valdemar continued his conquest in North Germany, Livonia, and Estonia, thus laying the groundwork for a second Danish empire (this one in the Baltic) and initiating a struggle which was to go on intermittently for the next seven hundred years.

Within Denmark itself, a dual struggle between king and nobility and between church and state continued unabated. Attempts to strengthen the royal power were countered by the nobles in 1282 when they obliged the king to sign the Danish equivalent of the Magna Carta. When this was violated, they went further and in 1319 established a Council of State without whose consent the king could not govern, make war, or (significantly) entrust any authority to German officers. The violation of this compact reopened the struggle, and both sides called upon the princes of North Germany for support. In the end, both king and nobility were the losers; the Count of Holstein was the victor. Not only did he appropriate all of Schleswig to his own domains, but he also proceeded to mortgage large parts of the kingdom to others, including the sale of Skåne to Sweden.

Lübeck and the other commercial towns of North Germany (that is, the Hanseatic League) were interested in breaking the power of the Count of Holstein, and to that end they financed the son of the last Danish king, one Valdemar Atterdag by name, in the repurchase of certain hereditary districts in northern Jutland. Within 14 years, Valdemar had shrewdly managed to reconstruct the Danish realm (largely through repurchase by installments), apart from Schleswig and Skåne. In 1360 he regained the latter province by force of arms, and the following year he went on to ravage the German trade center at Visby and capture the island of Gotland. The Hansa now realized that its support of Valdemar had been an unlucky investment, and it set about bringing him to terms. After a lengthy contest, the Danish Council of State was forced to sign the Peace of Stralsund in 1370. In it the Hansa was granted complete freedom of trade in Denmark, the right to veto the royal succession, and a guarantee of two-thirds of the revenues of Skåne for a period of 15 years. At the time, the herring fisheries off the south coast of Skåne were a veritable gold-mine, so this represented a major economic as well as political triumph for the League.

At this critical juncture, Denmark's destiny lay in the hands of a woman—Margrethe, daughter of Valdemar Atterdag. Margrethe had married Håkon VI, king of Norway, and upon the death of her father, their infant son Olaf was elected king of Denmark. When Håkon died in 1380, Olaf inherited the throne of Norway, thus forming a union between Denmark and Norway which was to endure over four hundred years. Because Håkon's father had also been king of Sweden, Margrethe had her son Olaf proclaimed heir to the Swedish throne in 1385. Olaf's premature death two years later did not deter Margrethe from pushing forward her grandiose plan for unifying all three Scandinavian kingdoms, and in 1388, with the help of the Swedish nobility, she ousted the German king of Sweden. In the process, however, she was forced to sacrifice Schleswig to the Count of Holstein in order to maintain peace on her southern frontier. In 1389 she had her grand-nephew, Erik of Pomerania, elected king of the three countries, but retained effective control of the realm until her death in 1412. Her formal effort to consolidate her tripartite kingdom was made in a draft presented in 1397 at the Swedish city of Kalmar, and although it was never ratified by the councils of the three states it worked relatively well as long as she lived.

As Margrethe's successor, Erik proved considerably less able. Indeed, he brought the Kalmar Union to the brink of ruin by attempting to retrieve Schleswig from Holstein. The Hansa threw its full support behind the Count of Holstein, not only helping him to reconquer all of Schleswig, but also blockading all three of the countries. The self-sufficient farming districts of Denmark and southern Sweden weathered the storm with little difficulty, but the mining areas of central Sweden, cut off from their markets, and Norway, lacking access to imported foodstuffs, were both stirred into open revolt. Erik was forced off the throne, and his cousin, Christopher of Bavaria, was elected king of all three realms. Christopher reigned only at the sufferance of the Hansa, for he was obliged to renew all of the League's trading privileges in Denmark, guarantee Schleswig to the Count of Holstein, and act only in accord with the three Councils of State, who thus exercised the real political control in the Union.

Christopher of Bavaria was succeeded on the throne by Christian of Oldenburg, a nephew of the Count of Holstein. His choice by the Danish Council of States seemed a particularly auspicious one, for when his uncle died the barons of Holstein chose Christian as their prince. This meant that both Schleswig and Holstein were reincorporated into the Danish realm. In fact, Christian was obliged to swear that Schleswig and Holstein should forever remain united —an oath which was to have far-reaching and totally unforeseen consequences.

In its eagerness to choose a successor who would best promote the interests of Denmark, the Danish Council of State had acted without consulting either the Swedish or Norwegian nobles. The latter were righteously offended, and they reacted by choosing a Swedish nobleman as their king. At this point the Church intervened and inspired a revolt which resulted in the ouster of the Swede and the coronation of Christian. But, despite the fact that Christian had the complete backing of the Hansa, he suffered an ignominious defeat at the hands of a Swedish peasant army in 1471. To his deathbed he carried a burning desire for revenge, urging his son Hans to renew the struggle on an even grander scale. But the time was not ripe, and Hans left the Union in a still weaker state when he died in 1513. It remained for his son, Christian II, to write the final chapter of Scandinavian Union. In a desperate effort to stamp out Swedish resistance, he landed in Stockholm in 1520 and had all the nationalist leaders executed. Rather than quell the revolt, however, this atrocity spurred it to new heights. Within three years the Danes had been driven out completely, and a free and independent Sweden had been proclaimed. Margrethe's dream of Scandinavian Union was finally laid to rest. The economic and political interests of Denmark and Sweden had proven too divergent to form a stable amalgam. Indeed, the political interests of Denmark and Norway seldom paralleled one another, either, but Norway lacked the economic strength to break away and stand on her own. This was conclusively demonstrated in 1536 when Christian III used the Reformation as an instrument to confiscate Church property, consolidate royal authority, and demote Norway from the status of an equal kingdom to that of a dependent territory.

THE SWEDISH CHALLENGE IN THE BALTIC

Denmark's greatest challenge had now shifted from its southern frontier and the German states to Sweden and the Baltic arena. Although the Danes had never been able to completely free themselves from German economic and political domination, both the Dutch (in 1441) and the English (10 years later) had broken the Hanseatic trade monopoly in the Baltic by breaching the Sound. This maritime competition and the upswing in commerce which it betokened both worked to the advantage of Denmark. Not only did it permit her greater freedom of action in the political sphere, but it also contributed considerable revenue to the royal treasury in the form of Sound Dues, first instituted in 1427 and collected at the fortress in Helsingör.

Strategically, Denmark had a much stronger position than did Sweden, as the struggle for the Baltic opened. In fact, Danish territories almost surrounded Sweden. On the west Norway stretched from the Arctic Ocean to the mouth of the Göta river and in one place (Jämtland) reached to within 30 miles of the Gulf of Bothnia. Though the Swedes had always managed to retain a "window to the west" at the Göta mouth, the territory of Denmark proper commenced immediately to the south, embracing the provinces of Halland, Skåne, and Blekinge on the Swedish mainland. Valdemar Atterdag's capture of Gotland outflanked the Swedish east coast, and the Danish seizure of Ösel, off the Estonian coast, and the district around Reval (modern Tallinn) posed a threat to the age-old Swedish trade route leading into the Gulf of Finland.

The opening round between the two contestants was the Scandinavian Seven Years' War which began in 1563. Most of the war was passed in a naval blockade of Sweden by the much superior Danish navy, though on land the Swedish army showed its strength by ravaging the border districts of Norway. Finally, in 1570, with both countries having been brought to the point of exhaustion, the struggle ended in a draw.

In order to rebuild her finances, Denmark revised the Sound Tolls so that they were levied as a duty on cargo rather than as a fixed charge per ship. This had the effect of tripling the revenues collected, and as commerce increased, Denmark entered an unparalleled age of prosperity. When Christian IV came to the throne in 1588, the country had no debt whatsoever. But the resumption of hostilities with Sweden in 1611 soon proved that while Denmark retained mastery of the sea, Sweden was growing ever stronger as a land power. The war was inconclusive, and the peace of 1613 effected no real change in the political balance between them.

At this point, however, the Dutch intervened by calling for free trade in the Baltic, and to that end they formed an alliance with Sweden and the North German towns against Denmark. Literally overnight Denmark had been transformed from the encircling power to the encircled, confronted by the Swedish army on the north and the powerful Dutch navy on the west. The outbreak of the Thirty Years' War in 1618 seemed to be Christian's only way out, and he went to the aid of the Protestant princes of North Germany. But all he reaped for his effort was one defeat after another, until in 1627 Catholic armies marched the length of Jutland and laid waste the entire peninsula. Two years later Christian had to withdraw from the struggle, and his dominions were returned only on the promise that he would abandon his allies.

Meanwhile, victorious Swedish armies were moving southward and westward along the shore of the Baltic. The Danes realized that Sweden's decision to enter the religious struggle was as much motivated by her desire to break the ring of Danish encirclement as it was to assist the Protestant cause. Denmark's only hope now was to gain time and rebuild her strength. One way to do this was to increase the Sound Tolls, an act which pushed the Dutch squarely into the arms of the Swedes. When Swedish forces finally could be diverted from their campaign to the south (1643), they marched through Holstein, Schleswig, and all of of Jutland as their Catholic rivals had done less than two decades earlier. On the mainland of Sweden nearly all of Skåne was conquered, and the Danish fleet was administered a staggering blow by a combined Dutch-Swedish armada off the southern islands of Denmark. When the Danes sued for peace in 1645, it was manifestly clear that the balance of power had shifted against them. By the terms of the treaty Denmark was forced to give up both Gotland and Ösel, thus losing her position on the eastern flank of Sweden, as well as Jämtland and Härjedalen, the most threatening positions on Sweden's western flank. Skåne was restored to Denmark, as was the Sound Toll, but not without granting Holland her point—a reduction of tariffs for Dutch ships. The death of Christian IV and the end of the bitter Thirty Years' War in 1648 found Denmark in a state of virtual ruin.

Continued Swedish successes in the eastern Baltic soon proved disquieting to the Dutch as well as the Danes, for they realized that their goal of free trade would be as much in jeopardy with the Swedes in complete control of the sea as it had been with the Danes in command. Thus, during the reign of Christian's successor, Frederick III, the Dutch realigned themselves on the side of Denmark against the Swedes. However, not until Frederick allied himself with Poland and Russia in 1657 did he give Sweden an excuse to extricate herself from a difficult campaign in the marshes of Poland and turn her full attention back to Denmark.

Once again Jutland was invaded from the south by Swedish armies, but the islands remained secure in the lee of the Danish Navy, at least until winter set in. Then the Swedes found an unexpected ally in the form of ice, which permitted them to cross the Little Belt to Fyn and the Great Belt to Lolland, Falster, and finally Sjaelland. When Swedish troops were within 15 miles of Copenhagen, the Danes once more had to sue for peace. This time the terms of the treaty were extremely harsh, for Denmark was forced to give up all of her provinces on the Swedish mainland, the Norwegian province of Bohuslän just north of the Göta river, the island of Bornholm in the Baltic, and the Tröndelag district of central Norway (cutting that country in half and giving Sweden access to the open Atlantic). Even so, had they wanted to, the Swedes could have extinguished the Danish state then and there. But, instead of counting themselves fortunate at getting off so lightly, the Danes immediately set about trying to sabotage the treaty. This so enraged the Swedish king that he launched a second invasion of Sjaelland in August 1658 and marched straight for Copenhagen. Now the burgomaster of the capital saw an opportunity for extorting a charter from the King which not only made Copenhagen a Free City, but also granted its residents the same privileges as the nobility. This secured, the people of Copenhagen put up such a defense that the Swedish armies were stopped in their tracks. The siege dragged on until a Dutch fleet forced the Swedish blockade to bring in supplies and Polish and German armies began to move into Jutland to assist Denmark. At this point the untimely death of the Swedish king provided a convenient signal for beginning peace talks, and these were ably conducted in behalf of Denmark by a nobleman named Hannibal Sehested.

During the negotiations, Sehested succeeded in regaining both the island of Bornholm and the Tröndelag district of Norway. However, pressure from the Dutch prompted him to give up all claims to Skåne. With opposing powers sharing the two sides of the Sound, Holland felt that a balance of power would finally be struck which would further her commercial interests in the Baltic. Sehested went on to set the stage for a total reorganization of the Danish administration and for a new departure in the country's foreign relations, especially vis-à-vis Sweden. The monarchy was thenceforward to be hereditary and absolute, rather than elective as through all of Denmark's previous history. He likewise believed that Denmark must face the fact that Sweden had now attained great-power status and that the only alternative to good relations with her northern neighbor was to be used as a pawn by the Dutch. He sharply curtailed the offensive army and concentrated instead on bolstering the country's defenses.

Sehested's foreign policy found little favor among the military, who wanted revenge on Sweden and the return of Skåne. They finally got their war from 1675 to 1679, but it was inconclusive. At last they had to bow to the will of France, Sweden's ally, and accept a 10-year alliance with their traditional enemy—one of the goals Sehested had sought.

However, accepting a position subordinate to Sweden was not something most Danes would do any longer than they thought they had to. In 1699 they launched an invasion of Holstein-Gottorp (a principality linked to Sweden by marriage) in order to recapture part of Schleswig and break Sweden's flanking position on the south. Though the campaign fared badly, Karl XII's disaster at Poltava in 1709 emboldened the Danes to declare war on Sweden itself, thus joining company with Russia, Poland, and Prussia. The war dragged on until 1720, at which time Denmark incorporated the remaining portion of Schleswig, obliged the Swedes to pay an indemnity, and reinstituted the Sound Tolls for Swedish ships. Denmark-Norway and Sweden had finally reached an equality born of exhaustion, but in the process the domination of the Baltic had eluded both of them.

The remainder of the eighteenth century was relatively quiet as far as Denmark's foreign affairs were concerned, but her domestic affairs continued in a state of ferment. Friendly relations with Russia, the new mistress of the Baltic, became the cornerstone of Danish policy, and to that end Denmark enunciated a doctrine of armed neutrality for her large merchant fleet. During the American Revolutionary War, the Danes propounded several basic resolutions which have since been incorporated into the body of international law—namely, that the oceans were free to the trade of all nations, that the flag covers the cargo (that is, neutral ships are free to carry cargo, apart from contraband, between belligerents), and that neutral ships cannot be denied access to ports and harbors that are not effectively blockaded. These declarations were put to the test by the British in 1801, when in a violent naval engagement in the harbor of Copenhagen, they forced Denmark to put an end to merchant convoys operating in defiance of their blockade of Napoleonic Europe. Then, in 1806, Napoleon and the Russian Czar agreed to set up a blockade of their own with the intention that Denmark-Norway's large merchant fleet be put at their disposal. Upon learning of the new French demands made upon Denmark, the British acted swiftly to prevent the Danish fleet from falling into Napoleon's hands. They surrounded Copenhagen and subjected it to two days of uninterrupted bombardment before the Danish navy was surrendered to them. Such overt aggression led the Danish King to join the war as an ally of Napoleon, a mistake which in the final peace settlement not only involved the loss of Norway to Sweden, but also of Pomerania to Prussia. As compensation, Denmark was awarded the small Duchy of Lauenberg adjacent to Holstein.

THE SCHLESWIG-HOLSTEIN ISSUE REVIVED

The idea of a unitary state—a state that incorporated more than one nationality into a single political entity—was given a severe setback by the loss of Norway. Then, after the 1830 revolution, the first demand was raised for a separate constitution for Schleswig-Holstein, linking the duchies merely in a personal union with the kingdom. The Danes reaffirmed their position that Schleswig and Holstein were Danish crown lands and must continue to be governed like the kingdom itself in a tripartite unitary state. However, the king did make a concession to more democratic government by establishing four consultative provincial diets—one for the islands, one for Jutland, and one each for Schleswig and Holstein.

Nevertheless, the growing enchantment of the German Holsteiners for the emerging Germanic Confederation soon led them to espouse the cause of Schleswig-Holstein's complete detachment from Denmark and union with the states to the south. By way of compromise, Danish liberals countered with the *Ejderdan* movement, whose aim was to incorporate Danish Schleswig as a province of the kingdom and to fix the country's southern boundary along the Eider river, thus giving up all claim to German Holstein. However, the Danish king and government would hear nothing of either suggestion, but insisted instead on the preservation of the tripartite unitary state.

Seeing Schleswig coming more and more under the domination of Holstein, the Danish liberals now began a policy of pan-Scandinavianism. They envisioned a union of the three Scandinavian countries, even if only temporary, to meet the growing menace of German expansion. Swedish support was enlisted by making the motto of the movement "Schleswig and Finland," for Sweden was still smarting from the loss of the latter country to Russia in 1809. However, pressure from the Russian government on both Denmark and Sweden obliged them to play down the movement.

The February Revolution of 1848 spurred the Holsteiners into again demanding a free joint constitution for Schleswig-Holstein. And once again the Ejderdan solution was raised by the Danish liberals. This time it received much greater support amongst the people, and a large unarmed crowd converged on the royal palace to demand a change of government and the implementation of this compromise policy. The king was persuaded against abdication by his advisers and convinced that he should become the leader of the movement rather than its victim. Thereupon the king announced that from that moment forward he regarded himself as a constitutional monarch and that a ministerial coalition (consisting of several liberals) would henceforth be responsible for the government of Denmark. Thus, the absolute monarchy of Denmark was dissolved as bloodlessly as it had been created less than two hundred years earlier.

The new government replied to the Holsteiners' demands by stating that Holstein could have a free constitution for itself, but that Schleswig was to be attached more closely to Denmark. Even before this reply had been received, however, the Holsteiners had revolted and set up a provisional government. A Danish conscript army was rushed to Schleswig to put down the uprising, and its initial victory convinced everyone that the war was already over. At this juncture, Prussia intervened, defeating the Danish army and driving deep into Jutland. England and Sweden-Norway adopted a wait-and-see attitude, but Russia did not. She did not want Prussia to acquire Kiel for use as a naval base, so after consultation with England she prompted Sweden-Norway into sending an expeditionary force into Fyn. At the same time she forwarded a note to Prussia requesting the latter's withdrawal from Jutland. This accomplished, the Great Powers lost interest in Denmark's cause, for they preferred to see the continuation of the old unitary state. Once Prussia had been forced out of the war, the Danish army went on to defeat the Holsteiners, who quickly sued for peace. A protocol was then drawn up and signed in London between the Scandinavian states and the non-German Great Powers. This guaranteed the indivisibility of the Danish realm in return for Denmark's promise not to attach Schleswig more closely to her than it was attached to Holstein—in other words, her promise not to disturb the status quo. Clearly the solution to the Schleswig-Holstein problem had not been found; it had only been postponed.

During the war, the foundations of modern Danish democracy were formally laid through the adoption of a new liberal constitution. However, when the Danish parliament unilaterally enacted a Joint Constitution for Holstein in 1855, the Holsteiners complained that they had not been consulted. Both Prussia and Austria seized on this action to denounce Denmark for having gone back on her word given in the London Protocol. This in turn inflamed the Ejderdanist movement once again. When the Diet of the German Confederation declared both Holstein's local constitution and the joint constitution invalid, the liberal-dominated government of Denmark acknowledged the decisions and rescinded them as they applied to Holstein. By this action, of course, Holstein was completely cut off from the constitutional life of Denmark. Thus, by acquiescing to German pressure, the Danish liberal government had shrewdly managed to move one step closer to quitting themselves entirely of Holstein—a basic aim of the Ejderdanist movement.

However, Denmark was not only under pressure by the Germans on her land frontier; she was also under pressure from the United States on her sea frontier. Since 1837, the Americans had increasingly challenged Denmark's right to levy dues on shipping passing through the Sound, claiming that it had no foundation in international law and that it interfered with free trade. After protracted negotiations, the Danes agreed to abolish the tolls in 1857, in return for compensation from the maritime powers using the Sound.

About the same time, the basis of Denmark's modern transportation system was being formed, and this, too, soon came to reflect the pressure of international politics. The country's first steamship line had been established from Copenhagen to Kiel, while the country's first railway was constructed from Kiel to Altona—in essence, a recognition of the undiminished importance of ancient isthmian trade-route and an encouragement to the industries of Holstein. As a result of the war of 1848-1850, however, the Danish liberal government sought to divert trade away from Holstein and Hamburg toward England instead. Hence, they wanted a transverse rail line across the islands to Jutland, where lines would fan out to several North Sea ports. The Jutlanders, on the other hand, wanted direct rail lines south to their traditional livestock markets in the Duchies and in Germany. Finally, in the early 1860's a compromise was worked out which included both the transverse line across the islands and two north-south lines in Jutland, one along each side of the peninsula.

At the same time, the Danish liberal government was stepping up its program of Danification in central and southern Schleswig, and in 1863 it felt that the time was ripe to offer Holstein a new constitution of its own and to extend a new joint constitution to Schleswig. Bismarck, the Prussian minister of state, immediately accused Denmark of having broken its pledge given at the end of the 1848-1850 war, and he got Austria to agree that Holstein and south Schleswig should be taken from her. The Danish liberal government was put under pressure both by the signatories of the London Protocol and by its political adversaries at home to back down, but it refused. German troops then proceeded to occupy Holstein, and on February 1, 1864 they crossed the Eider into Schleswig. The marshes flanking the Dannevirke were frozen, so that the Danish army had to draw back into north Schleswig to make a stand. Although they heroically held the Germans at bay for over six weeks, the outcome was never in doubt, and finally the Germans stormed into northern Jutland. Even so, when peace negotiations were commenced, the Danish liberal government proved so intransigent that several opportunities for compromise were rejected. When at last the liberals were forced to resign, the conservative government which took over had no leverage for bargaining at all, and not only Holstein but nearly all of Schleswig as well had to be surrendered to the Germans. Thus, one-third of Denmark's national territory and 40 percent of her population (including 200,000 ethnic Danes) were lost, with the result that the German border now encircled the ancient town of Ribe and extended to the Little Belt.

THE EMERGENCE OF MODERN DENMARK

This crushing defeat shook Denmark to its very foundations. Liberalism was discredited, and as political reaction swept the country, a new and highly conservative constitution was promulgated. The year 1866 also saw the establishment of the Society for the Cultivation of Heaths, an instrumentality designed to further "internal colonization," especially in western Jutland. Now that Denmark had lost such a sizable proportion of her cultivable area, she felt that she must more intensively utilize that which remained. About the same time, improvements in transportation (in particular the opening of the Suez Canal and the penetration of railways into the continental heartlands) began having their effects on Danish agriculture. Grain could no longer be grown in competition with the Ukraine, America, and Australia; if Denmark was to maintain a viable agricultural economy, she would have to concentrate on what she could do best. This meant specializing in livestock products such as butter, cheese, meat, and eggs. A transformation as radical as this required a concerted program of rural education, a purpose for which the recently founded "peoples' high schools" served admirably. It also required great capital investment, which individual farmers were in no position to undertake; yet, by pooling their resources and labor, the farmers were able to avail themselves of the most modern technological innovations and the most advanced scientific methods. In anticipation of a growing export of Danish agricultural products to England, a new port was created on the west coast of Jutland where, in 1868, the groundwork was laid for Esbjerg, now the country's fourth largest city. Thus, the latter decades of the nineteenth century saw not only a striking transformation of the Danish economy, but also the steady growth of the cooperative movement, and with it, Danish social and political democracy. A new, broadly-based prosperity had come into being as Danish farms increasingly turned their attention to providing foodstuffs for the growing industrial nations of Britain and Germany.

Nevertheless, despite the progress which was being made in the country's domestic affairs, Denmark's international position remained as difficult and precarious as ever. After the Franco-Prussian War, Germany was the master of the continent, and in Schleswig a Germanization policy was pushed with vigor and violence. When Denmark tried to intercede in behalf of her expatriate countrymen, she was told that she must suppress her anti-German newspapers and that in the event of a European war, Denmark would have to close the Great Belt with German assistance. She was also told that any revision of the Schleswig frontier would only be "thinkable" after an alliance with Germany in the future war and that she must put her defenses in order so as to keep out the English. If Denmark was either unable or unwilling to defend herself from the English, the Germans "would have to see to it themselves."

At the outbreak of World War I, Denmark declared her neutrality in concert with Norway and Sweden. Yet, when hostilities began between England and Germany, the Germans mined the waters south of the Great Belt and insisted that Denmark mine the Great

Belt itself. Reluctantly they proceeded to do so, informing England of the impossible situation in which they found themselves and receiving a very sympathetic reply in return.

Politically, the years of World War I saw rapid changes in Denmark. A more liberal constitution was adopted, suffrage became almost universal, representative parliamentary government was established, the judicial system was democratized, Denmark's last tropical colony (the Virgin Islands) was sold to the United States, and Iceland was granted recognition as a sovereign country in personal union with the King of Denmark. Following the war, the Allies granted a Danish demand for a free plebiscite in Schleswig. When the results were in, North Schleswig (with an 80 percent Danish vote) was returned to Denmark, while central Schleswig (with a correspondingly high vote for the Germans) was left to Germany. Thus, the present boundary between the two countries has been in existence only since 1920.

The war and its aftermath caused serious repercussions in the Danish economy which were further aggravated by the Great Depression. Both Germany and England placed restrictions on Danish exports, agricultural prices plummeted, and unemployment rose steadily. As militant Nazism began raising a new spectre to the south, the major Danish political parties effected a conciliation which paved the way not only for labor peace, but also for an accelerated program of social reform. However, when England concluded a naval treaty with Germany in 1935 wherein she relinquished the Baltic to the Nazi sphere of influence, Denmark's international position once again appeared hopeless. Thus, Denmark's only course was to accept Hitler's non-aggression treaty proffered in the spring of 1939, though Norway, Sweden, and Finland felt themselves secure enough to decline. The treaty's worthlessness was revealed early in the morning of April 9, 1940, when the military, naval, and air forces of the Third Reich occupied Denmark and received its capitulation in two and a half hours.

By the terms of the capitulation, Denmark's government was to remain in the hands of the king and cabinet. But Hitler's assertion that Denmark was a "model protectorate" took on an ever more hollow ring as the Danish underground movement organized itself and began an intensive campaign of sabotage. By August 1943 the Nazis gave up every pretext of trying to "do business" with the Danes and seized control of the country's entire administrative apparatus. However, with just a few minutes warning the Danes managed to scuttle their entire navy in the harbor of Copenhagen. Similarly, when the Nazis attempted to round up the country's Jewish colony for deportation to the gas chambers in October 1943, the Danish populace swiftly put them in hiding and managed to smuggle 90 percent of them to safety in Sweden.

The collapse of Nazi Germany in May 1945 heralded the emergence of a new power in the Baltic, the Soviet Union. Indeed, it was the Russians who "liberated" the island of Bornholm from the Germans. Pro-Russian feeling was at an all-time high in postwar Denmark, as evidenced by the election of 18 Communist members to parliament in October 1945. Yet, as Stalin's satellization policy began to unfold in eastern and central Europe, Danish public opinion cooled rapidly, and Denmark entered into NATO as a charter member in 1949. Since that time Denmark has actively supported NATO, but like Norway has refused to allow foreign military forces and/or nuclear weapons to be stationed on her soil. However, Greenland affords something of an exception, for during World War II the Danish minister in Washington permitted the United States to build and maintain airbases there, and in 1952 the Danish government agreed to allow construction of a major Strategic Air Command base and a ballistic missile early warning station (BMEWS) at Thule in the far northwest. In 1953, when the Danish parliament was reconstituted as a unicameral house, Greenland was made an administrative county of Denmark with representation in the *Folketing,* and, in that sense a foreign base can be said to exist on Danish soil. In the air and missile age Greenland occupies as strategic a position in the "Arctic Mediterranean" as Denmark itself has occupied in ages past between the North and Baltic Seas. One can only hope that Greenland will be spared the confused and troubled evolution with which Denmark's location has saddled her.

Just as Denmark's geopolitical position has been difficult throughout the country's history, its economic equilibrium promises to become increasingly precarious in a Europe divided into rival trading blocs. The two most important buyers of Danish agricultural commodities are West Germany and the United Kingdom, one a member of the European Economic Community, or "Common Market," and the other, the cornerstone of the European Free Trade Association. Although an active member of the latter group, Denmark cannot be excluded from the former without experiencing serious repercussions. Hence, total economic integration of western Europe is a goal to which the Danes ascribe the highest priority. At the same time, of course, they realize that their bargaining position is an extremely delicate one, for in both blocs there has been a certain reluctance to extend free trade provisions to agricultural products. The Danes have no fear that they cannot compete on their own merits; all they ask is to be allowed to enter into the competition freely and fairly, without artificial economic or political restraint. But, in a world still dominated by nationalistic rivalries, even this may be too much to expect—or even to ask.

THE first political entities to arise within the present boundaries of Norway were tribal kingdoms which began to take form in the broad, open valleys of the east during the early centuries of the Christian era. Somewhat later, independent peasant republics emerged in the higher valleys of Oppland and in the lowlands of Tröndelag adjacent to Trondheimsfjord. However, along the dissected western coast, little political consolidation was achieved until the period of the Great Migrations when the Hords and the Rygers arrived by sea from north Germany and subjugated the earlier inhabitants. At any rate, well before the Vikings erupted onto the pages of European history, the coastal districts from the mouth of Oslofjord to beyond the Arctic Circle had come to be known by a common designation, even though they still lacked a common political allegiance. *Norvegr,* or "The Northern Way," with its host of petty kingdoms, had no central focus until one was provided in the person of a king who commanded the entire region. It is interesting that such central direction did not develop within the coastal region itself, but rather was imposed upon it from the eastern valleys by way of the lowlands of Tröndelag. By mounting a vigorous military campaign to the north, west, and south, King Harald the Fair-Haired finally succeeded in winning the allegiance of all the petty kings and chieftains. Although there was no fixed capital as such, the king resided most of the time on a large estate outside present-day Trondheim. Perhaps the fact of sheer distance encouraged tribal uprisings against him in the south, for the Hords, Ryger, Egder, and Teler soon rose in rebellion. Meeting them in combat at Hafursfjord (near modern Stavanger), Harald decisively defeated the southern chieftains in the year 872. It is from this date that Norway traces her emergence as a unified nation-state.

THE RISE AND DECLINE
OF THE NORWEGIAN EMPIRE

However, many of the southern chieftains preferred exile to subordination, and with their retinues they set sail for the Shetlands, Orkneys, Hebrides, Faeroes, and Iceland. Those who settled within striking distance of the Norwegian coast did not miss an opportunity to harass their homeland with Viking raids each summer. Ultimately Harald was obliged to return the harassment to their own shores, and finally, by crushing their opposition and winning their allegiance, he incorporated the first overseas territories into the Norwegian realm.

To be sure, the depredations of the Viking age involved far more than struggles between the Northmen themselves, for already before the year 800 they had discovered that Christian Europe was largely unable to protect the wealth that it was beginning to amass. Churches, with their riches of gold and silver, became prime targets of these summer forays, and many slaves were taken, also. Few towns accessible to the sea escaped their hit-and-run plundering, and eventually many areas of attractive farmland were annexed and permanently settled by the Norse in places ranging from Ireland to Sicily.

These voyages of pillage and conquest did not come to an end until Norway was itself incorporated into the fold of Latin Christendom. By the year 1000 King Olav Trygvesson had obliged the chieftains throughout the realm to submit to baptism and had established a settlement at the mouth of the river Nid—Nidaros, now Trondheim—as his seat of government. A couple of decades later a royal manor was constructed in Nidaros by King Olav Haraldsson, and following his death in the battle of Stiklestad (1030) and later canonization as the patron saint of Norway, he was buried in the town. Near the site of his grave the Nidaros Cathedral was erected, a magnificent Gothic structure that became the archepiscopal see of the entire North Atlantic region in 1153 and the goal of pilgrims through the Middle Ages. Nidaros thus emerged as the first "capital" and the principal ecclesiastic center of an empire that extended from the Göta river in the south to the Arctic Ocean in the north and embraced the outer islands of Scotland as well. Its religious sphere was vaster than its political dominion, however, for in addition to four bishoprics within Norway itself (namely Stavanger, Bergen, Oslo, and Hamar) it had authority over six bishoprics in the western islands (including those in Iceland and Greenland.)

Already by the beginning of the twelfth century, the church had become the largest landowner in Norway, and the introduction of tithing about that time further enhanced its wealth and authority. Church and state grew hand in hand, with a structured, feudalistic society of titled landowners and ecclesiastics gradually submerging the independent freeholders. While religious affairs had found a geographic focus on Nidaros, the country's only political "center" remained the king, who alternately resided in Nidaros, Bergen, and Oslo. The formal creation of a hereditary monarchy in 1163 (replacing the elective monarchy of earlier times) was supported by the church as a stabilizing influence on the political life of the country.

In the century which followed, Norway rose to the height of its power, expanding its dominion to both the north and west. By 1252 a northern boundary with Novgorod had been fixed at Lyngenfjord, although territories as far east as the White Sea were administered jointly by both powers. Within another decade, Iceland and Greenland were incorporated into the realm, although about the same time the Hebrides were lost. A political empire that spanned the North Atlantic as widely as did the religious authority of Nidaros had finally been achieved.

However, Norway's greatness was extremely short-lived, for during the following century the country suffered a number of serious reverses. By 1285 the Hanseatic League had succeeded in reducing the western and northern regions to the status of economic vassalage, due to its monopoly of the fish and grain trade through Bergen.

In 1319 the death of Håkon V terminated the royal line of Norway, and the throne passed first to the Swedish court and later to the Danish. In 1349 the Black Death scourged the country so thoroughly that many areas were virtually depopulated. As a result, land rentals contracted sharply, labor was hard to come by, and a general economic depression set in.

It is ironic that, just as the country's fortunes began to wane, a fixed political capital emerged in Oslo. From about 1300 on, Akershus fortress, the strongest fortified point in Norway, became the principal residence of the king. Though this later facilitated control of the country by the Swedish and Danish crowns, respectively, it was still necessary for each monarch of Norway to journey to Nidaros for his corontation. Even after the king of Denmark reduced Norway from the status of an equal kingdom to that of a dependent territory in 1536 (largely through the vehicle of the Reformation), part of the price that the Danish ruler was obliged to pay for the country's allegiance was the arduous junket across the Dovre mountains to the great cathedral.

THE EVOLUTION OF NORWAY'S BOUNDARIES

Norway's location proved to be sufficiently offside through most of history to insulate her from involvement in the political expansion of other European states. On her sea frontier, which led northeastward into the Arctic Ocean and the White Sea, Norway met no organized challenge except from the Russians. Early in the 1300's the Norwegians built a church and fortress at Vardö to serve as an administrative center for collecting taxes from the Lapps. The first Russian settlement on the north coast of the Kola Peninsula was made in 1524, but Novgorod had also been taxing the Lapps as far west as Lyngenfjord since the early fourteenth century. Swedish tax-collectors, moving north from the Gulf of Bothnia, likewise managed to extract tribute from many of the interior Lapps, so these hapless people often found themselves paying two and three levies a year. About the beginning of the seventeenth century, spheres of influence began to crystallize more sharply within the region. The Russians collected their last Lapp tax in Finnmark in 1600, and the last Norwegian tribute was extracted from the Kola Lapps a dozen years later. The Neiden, Pasvik, and Pechenga areas remained the only common districts between the Norwegians and the Russians, though the Inari district was common to them and the Swedes as well, and in the "South Mountain" district (interior Finnmark) Norway shared tax privileges with Sweden.

The long land frontier which separated Norway from Sweden through the length of the Scandinavian Peninsula was seldom a source of concern to either country. The national energies of the Norwegians were primarily directed toward the open sea to the west and north, while the Swedes turned their attention principally to the east across the Baltic. The undefined boundary between the two peoples ran through sparsely inhabited forests and mountains, and the political allegiance of any given district along the border depended solely on ease of access to the east or west. Thus the provinces of Jämtland and Härjedalen were historically oriented westward to Norway via the Jämtland Gap rather than southward through the forests to Sweden.

After Sweden broke out of the Danish sponsored "Kalmar Union" and Norway was reduced to the status of a dependent territory of Denmark, Norway suffered from Swedish invasions whenever a conflict broke out between the two countries. In the Seven Years' War (1563-1570), Swedish armies laid waste the eastern districts of Norway, burning the towns of Sarpsborg, Hamar, and Trondheim. However, no boundary change resulted, for the principal struggle was the contest for naval supremacy in the Baltic, rather than for military supremacy within the Scandinavian Peninsula. A hundred years later (1658-1660) Swedish armies permanently detached the province of Bohuslän from Denmark-Norway, thus breaking the only land link between the two parts of the realm. Jämtland and Härjedalen were also annexed by Sweden, but Tröndelag was returned following two years of Swedish occupation, no doubt because it represented an untenable *Wachstumspitze* ("point of growth") in a direction in which she was not really interested in expanding.

Swedish military successes on land gave the Danes a belated awareness of the poor state of their defenses in the eastern border zone of Norway, and a crash program of fortress building was undertaken. Kongsten fortress was erected in Fredrikstad, the town which replaced the destroyed Sarpsborg; Fredriksten fortress was constructed on the heights overlooking Halden; and Kristiansten fortress was built on the hills above Trondheim. It is interesting to note that the only Norwegian town which was itself founded as a Danish military strongpoint is the city of Kristiansand. By decree of Christian IV it was established as a naval base in 1641, due to its strategic location near the entrance to the Skagerrak.

The new defenses effectively proved themselves when the Swedes invaded Norway during the war of 1709-1720, and thirty years later (1751) a fixed boundary was agreed upon by the two states and delimited in the field. No changes have since been made in it, although in the far north sovereignty over the one side of the line has been exchanged among the Swedes, Russians, and Finns. Norway's final boundary settlement was reached in 1826 when the last common districts along the Arctic coast were partitioned with the Russians. The Neiden and Pasvik districts went to Norway, while the Pechenga was allocated to Russia. Although the Pasvik river was chosen as the boundary, the Russians claimed and were given title to a small Greek Orthodox church which stood on the west bank of the river at Boris Gleb. This tiny outlier has subsequently proven just big enough to pose a complication in the use of the river for floating timber and generating power.

ADVANCE TOWARD INDEPENDENCE

Although Norway suffered little from direct military action during the Napoleonic Wars, the country nonetheless became a casualty of the conflict. The British maritime blockade succeeded in breaking the Danish supply lines to the country, with the result that the years from 1807 to 1814 were marked by severe privation and even famine. The blockade also had the effect of giving Norway a voice in the conduct of her own foreign affairs, an independence which she exercised briefly from 1809 until 1812. By the Peace of Kiel signed on January 14, 1814, Norway was taken from Denmark and given to Sweden. Christian Frederik, the heir to the throne of Denmark-Norway, was acting as Viceroy at the time, and his first reaction to the news was to name himself absolute monarch of an independent Norwegian state. However, Norwegian statesmen advised against such a move and asked him to summon a constitutional convention instead. Agreeing to recognize the sovereignty of the people, Christian Frederik convened an assembly at Eidsvoll on April 10. Five weeks later, on May 17, the Constitution was proclaimed and Christian Frederik was elected king. However, once the military campaign against Napoleon was concluded, the Swedes, with the backing of the Great Powers, demanded that the terms of the Kiel Treaty be observed. Norway refused, and on July 27 Swedish armies moved against the country. It was a hopeless struggle from the outset, and on August 14 the Norwegians signed an armistice at the Oslofjord town of Moss. The so-called Convention of Moss stipulated the summoning of an extraordinary Storting (parliament), in order to pass a law sanctioning the union of Norway with Sweden. It also stated that the Constitution was to remain in force, but that Christian Frederik must abdicate and leave the country. The Storting voted to approve the Union in November, and early the following year a separate agreement known as the Act of Union came into effect.

After its long domination by Denmark and its brief taste of independence in 1814, Norway used every device at its command to gain greater control over its own affairs. In 1837 municipal self-government was introduced. In 1848 a Norwegian political labor movement came into being. In 1869 an annual Storting, rather than the previous triennial parliament, was instituted. The latter body also restricted the access of governmental ministers to its debates by a resolution in 1872. This action, in turn, led to a prolonged and bitter struggle over the so-called "Veto-Issue," which was finally resolved in 1884 by the King recognizing the Storting as the decisive governing body in Norway and appointing a cabinet from among its leaders. It is to this event and date that Norway's first political parties, the Left (Liberal) and the Right (Conservative), trace their origins. Three years later, the Radical Left split off to form the Labor Party.

Ultimately, the issue which was to bring down the Union was that of a separate Norwegian consular service. The growth of Norwegian shipping interests necessitated a degree of foreign representation which the Swedish consular service was unable and unwilling to provide. Yet, time after time, the Swedish King vetoed resolutions by the Storting which would have created a separate Norwegian service, seeing in such a move the first step toward a completely independent foreign policy. Finally, the refusal of King Oscar II to either sanction the Storting's resolution or to accept the resignation of the Cabinet provoked a government crisis. When the Cabinet tried to turn its authority over to the Storting, the latter requested that the Cabinet stay in office and thereupon declared the union with Sweden dissolved.

For a time it appeared as though Sweden would resort to force to preserve the Union, but instead the King called for a referendum. The Norwegian electorate voted overwhelmingly in support of the Storting's resolution, and after lengthy negotiations in the Swedish border city of Karlstad, all outstanding differences were settled and the two countries parted in peace. As an act of courtesy and good will, the Norwegians offered their throne to a Swedish prince, but he refused. The Storting thereupon invited Prince Carl of Denmark to become King of Norway, and he accepted, with one reservation —that the people of Norway express themselves in favor of a monarchy rather than a republic. This the Norwegian electorate did by a wide majority, and on November 25, 1905, the popularly elected king arrived in Norway with his wife and infant son. He assumed the title of Haakon VII, a name last held by a Norwegian monarch in the fourteenth century, and his son was baptized with the equally historic name of Olav. For the first time in over five centuries, Norway was a free and sovereign country.

THE ECONOMIC AND POLITICAL EVOLUTION OF MODERN NORWAY

During the latter half of the nineteenth century, a revolution began in the economy of Norway as well as in her political life. The growth of shipping and industry and the improvement of transport and communications were mirrored in an accelerated movement of people from the farms to the towns. However, this economic expansion was not rapid enough to absorb the growing population of the country, and through the 1880's a swelling tide of Norwegians emigrated to the United States. It is nevertheless significant that on the eve of her political independence Norway was riding the greatest wave of prosperity she had ever known.

Although much had already been accomplished, much more remained for the new nation to do. Not until 1909 was a railway completed across the mountains linking Oslo (then Kristiania) and Bergen. This masterpiece of engineering remains to this day the only all-land, all-year connection between the country's two largest cities, for most transmontane highways are blocked by snow for six or seven months of the year. Although a devious, narrow-gauge rail link had been forged between Oslo and Trondheim in 1877 (by way of Österdal), it was not until 1921 that a continuous standard-gauge line joined the two cities by the more direct and historic "coronation" route of Gudbrandsdal. The south coast city of Kristiansand could not be reached by rail from the capital until 1935, and the first train to connect Oslo with Stavanger ran in part over a shoddy Nazi-built roadbed finished in 1944. Northward a rail tentacle had been pushed to Namsos by 1934, to Mosjöen by 1940, to the Arctic Circle by the end of the war, and into Bodö only in 1962. Beyond Bodö, Highway 50 provides the sole overland artery into the Arctic provinces, and even it is broken by several ferry crossings and is not continuously passable in winter. Narvik, North Norway's largest city, owes its existence to its ice-free harbor and the heavy-duty electric railway which links it with the iron mines of Swedish Lappland. Along the coast, daily express steamers maintain service between Bergen and Kirkenes on a schedule of four and a half days each way. With the coming of the airplane, travel time along the length of Norway has been cut to a matter of hours, and Bodö has developed into a major airport, capable of handling transpolar flights.

As was to be expected, the transformation of Norway into an urban-industrial society was accompanied by fundamental changes of political orientation within the country. For instance, by 1920 the people of the rural areas saw the growth of towns as so great a threat that they formed the Agrarian party to represent the political interests of the farmers. Their chief strength derived from the predominantly agricultural districts of eastern and central Norway. But, as the cities grew inexorably larger and more powerful, the Agrarians came to realize that they must broaden their appeal within the urban areas or perish. Thus, from 1961 they have called themselves the Center party.

The appeal of the Labor party grew steadily as industry and commerce expanded. The success of the Bolshevik revolution in Russia strengthened the more radical faction, and in 1921 a group of moderates broke away to form the Social Democratic party. When the Labor party severed relations with the Third International in 1923, the radicals bolted and established a separate Communist party. In 1927 the Social Democrats rejoined the Labor party, and from 1933 on, this revitalized party has constituted the largest single political movement in Norway. Its principal support is derived from industrial workers in the towns of eastern Norway and Tröndelag, but it likewise has a broad appeal among forest workers in the east and fishermen in the north. Geographically, the Communist party shows a similar distribution, though it has never captured as much as 14 percent of the popular vote and in most elections it has had to content itself with less than 5 percent of the ballots.

Norway's second largest political party, the Conservative, has its strongest appeal among the larger land owners, the shipping and whaling interests, and the managerial elements in the towns. As a result, its votes tend to be concentrated in Oslo, the prosperous county of Vestfold (on the west side of Oslofjord), and in the shipping towns of the south coast.

Two other of Norway's political parties show strong regional identification with the south and west. They are the older Liberal party, which has displayed a general weakening through the years, and the younger Christian Peoples' party, which has replaced it as the country's third largest political group.

Since 1935, however, the party which has consistently formed the government of Norway has been Labor. In the more than a quarter century during which it has fashioned Norway into a welfare state, the Labor party has shared power with its opponents once and has briefly been ousted from office once. During the Nazi occupation from 1940 to 1945, a coalition government in exile rallied Norwegian resistance against the Germans. And for about a month in the autumn of 1963, a non-Labor coalition took office, after Labor lost a vote of confidence in the Storting. It is significant that both of these lapses in Labor government can be attributed to international issues rather than domestic ones.

POSTWAR ISSUES

The shock of the German invasion and the ordeal of the Nazi occupation so indelibly inscribed themselves on the psyche of Norway that their memory continues to mold the country's foreign policy to this day. For example, most Norwegians have dismissed as an illusion the thought that their small country can any longer pursue a course of neutralism. Postwar attempts to form a Scandinavian defense alliance promised little security; hence, in April 1949 Norway became a charter member of NATO. At the same time, a deep and lingering distrust of the Germans colors Norway's relations with the country which has since become NATO's European cornerstone. Norway's experience with occupation forces has caused her to reject all NATO attempts to establish foreign military bases on her soil, although the NATO Northern Command has its headquarters at Kolsås just outside Oslo. As the only member of NATO (apart from Turkey) which has a common border with the Soviet Union, Norway has taken great pains to assure her Russian neighbor of the defensive nature of the pact. And, in keeping with her belief in the desirability of avoiding nuclear proliferation, Norway has likewise refused to allow any atomic weapons or missile delivery systems to be stockpiled on her territory.

However, a growing number of Norwegians see the advance of weapons technology as a diminution of their country's strategic importance and an increasing futility in attempting to build and maintain any kind of a meaningful defense. These sentiments found political expression in the parliamentary election of 1961 when two former members of the Labor party were elected to represent a new splinter group called the Socialist Peoples' party. This party not only advocates Norway's withdrawal from NATO, but also its taking steps toward total disarmament. As an illustration of its "balance of power" position, the two Socialist Peoples' representatives joined those of the opposition parties against Labor on a no confidence motion in August 1963 and brought down the government. A month later, when the non-Socialist coalition cabinet brought in its program, the Socialist Peoples' members switched to the side of Labor again, and returned the Labor government to office. Thus, while its domestic program continues to have the backing of a majority of the Storting, Labor's international policies have generated enough dissension to challenge the government's continued existence.

If this challenge is serious now, as a result of the nuclear issue, it promises to become even more serious at such time as Norway applies for membership in the Common Market. This is because Norway's offside location and marginal resource base will put her at the greatest relative disadvantage of any country in western Europe, save possibly Iceland. Particularly her agriculture and home-market industry will find difficulty in meeting the competition of better-endowed regions to the south. Even as it is, Norway has not achieved her high standard of living from her land alone, for in most years she can pay for only two-thirds of what she imports with what she exports. The gap in the country's balance of payments is closed by the earnings of her great merchant fleet—the most modern of the Big Three (the United States, the United Kingdom, and Norway)—and of her Antarctic whaling expeditions. Not without good reason has Norway's mercantile navy been termed her "floating empire": it spells the difference between economic success and failure, between prosperity and privation. But it also points up Norway's sensitivity to unfair competition (i.e., the "flags of convenience") and to discriminatory shipping practices (i.e., "half of U.S. trade in U.S. bottoms"). Thus, Norway finds herself in the difficult posture of championing free trade and freedom of the seas, while at the same time asking special concessions from the European Economic Community as a precondition for her eventual association with that group. Her dilemma is that of a small and basically poor country struggling for survival in a world where economic and political power belong to larger, richer, and usually indifferent states.

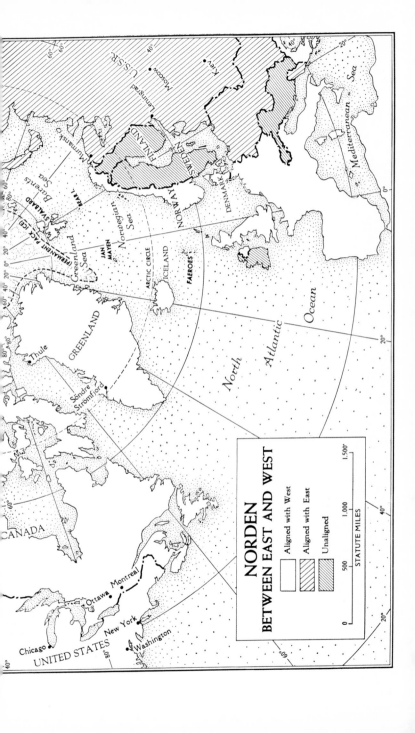

NORDEN
BETWEEN EAST AND WEST

Aligned with West
Aligned with East
Unaligned

STATUTE MILES

0   500   1,000   1,500

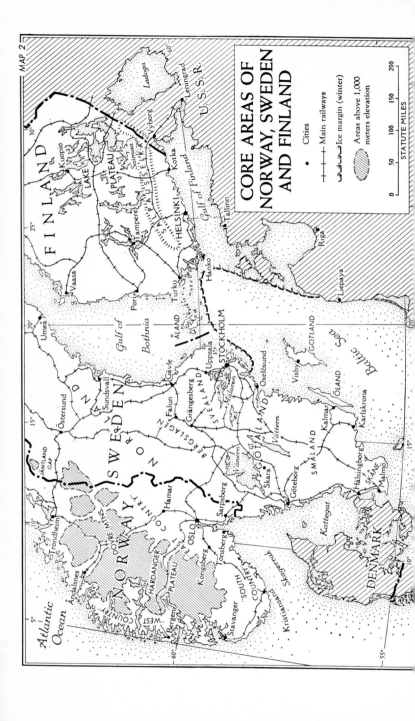

MAP 2

CORE AREAS OF
NORWAY, SWEDEN
AND FINLAND

• Cities
┼┼┼┼ Main railways
╍╍╍ Ice margin (winter)
▨ Areas above 1,000
meters elevation

0   50   100   150   200
STATUTE MILES

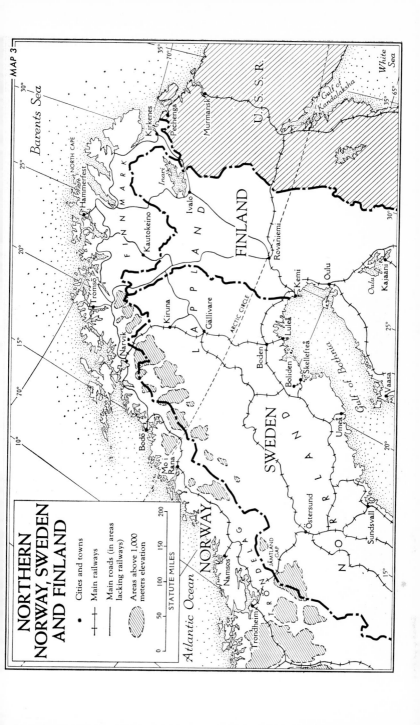

MAP 3

NORTHERN
NORWAY, SWEDEN
AND FINLAND

• Cities and towns
+++ Main railways
— Main roads (in areas
    lacking railways)
▨ Areas above 1,000
    meters elevation

STATUTE MILES
0   50   100   150   200

Barents Sea

U.S.S.R.

White Sea

Gulf of Kandalaksha

NORTH CAPE
Hammerfest
Kirkenes
Pechenga
Murmansk

F I N N M A R K

Tromsö
Kautokeino
Inari
Ivalo

FINLAND

L A P L A N D

Narvik
Kiruna
Gallivare
Rovaniemi
Kemi
Oulu
Kajaani

ARCTIC CIRCLE

Bodö
Moi Rana
Boden
Boliden
Luleå
Skellefteå

SWEDEN

N O R R L A N D

Umeå
Vaasa

Gulf of Bothnia

Atlantic Ocean

NORWAY

Namsos

Östersund

Sundsvall

JÄMTLAND
GAP

T R O N D E L A G

Trondheim

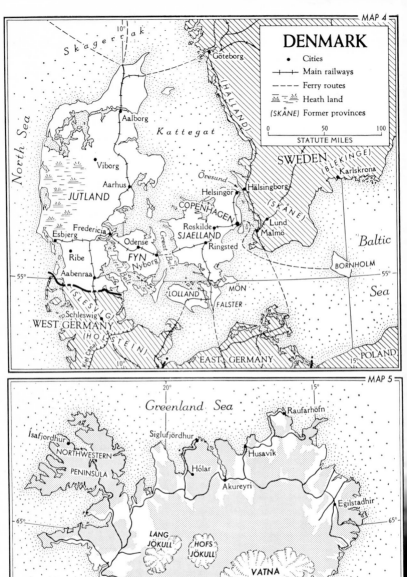

MAP 4

DENNMARK

- Cities
- Main railways
- Ferry routes
- Heath land
- (SKÅNE) Former provinces

0   50   100
STATUTE MILES

Skagerrak

North Sea

Göteborg

(HALLAND)

Kattegat

Aalborg

SWEDEN

(BLEKINGE)

Karlskrona

Viborg

Aarhus

Öresund

Helsingör   Hälsingborg

COPENHAGEN

(SKÅNE)

JUTLAND

Fredericia

Esbjerg

Roskilde   Lund
SJAELLAND   Malmö

Ringsted

Odense

Ribe

FYN

Nyborg

Baltic

Aabenraa

(SLESVIG)

Great Belt

Little Belt

MÖN

(LOLLAND)   FALSTER

BORNHOLM

Sea

WEST GERMANY

Schleswig

(HOLSTEIN)

Kiel Canal

EAST GERMANY

POLAND

MAP 5

Greenland Sea

Raufarhöfn

Ísafjordhur

Siglufjördhur

NORTHWESTERN

Husavík

PENINSULA

Hólar

Akureyri

Egilstadhir

LANG
JÖKULL

HOFS
JÖKULL

VATNA
JÖKULL

REYKJAVÍK   Thingvellir

Höfn

Skálholt

Laki
Volcano

Keflavík
(Main
U.S. base)

SOUTHERN

LOWLANDS

MYRDALS
JÖKULL

Vestmannaeyjar

Vík

ICELAND

- Towns and settlements
- Main roads
- Glaciers
- Wasteland

0   50   100
STATUTE MILES

Atlantic Ocean

5 Sweden: The Neutral Fulcrum

THE three golden crowns that constitute the national insignia of Sweden symbolize the original tripartite division of the realm. One crown represents *Svealand*, "The Land of the Svear," a region centered on Lake Mälaren in east-central Sweden. (The Swedish name for Sweden, *Sverige*, comes from the words *Svea rike*, meaning "Kingdom of the Svear.") The second crown represents *Götaland*, "The Land of the Goths," a region bordering the great lakes of south-central Sweden. And the third crown represents *Norrland*, or "Northland," a vast region of rolling forests that stretches away toward the north. The latter has always been Sweden's frontier—by far the largest region in area, but the one with the most severe climate, the poorest soils, and hence, the fewest people. Svealand and Götaland, in contrast, both gave rise to a relatively dense agricultural settlement at an early date, thanks to their warmer climate and the fact that they consisted largely of old lake plains with rather productive clay soils.

Just as the forested wilderness of Norrland long remained a "no man's land," so did the block-fault hills that trend east-west across the central Swedish lowland constitute population voids. Though few of them are very high, their ancient crystalline bedrock, steep slopes, and dense forest cover effectively discouraged the spread of settlement. As a result, they soon came to be recognized as "natural" boundaries between the Svear and the Goths. The ridge known as Kolmården (558 feet) marked the boundary between the Svear and the East Goths, while that called Tiveden (803 feet) defined the territorial limits of the Svear and the West Goths.

Although these tribes were closely related in blood and in culture, they were not politically united until sometime in the seventh century. Nevertheless, among both the Svear and the Goths a form of representative government was so firmly established before unification that it continued to manifest itself long afterwards. Each head of a family belonged to a clan and several clans formed a *härad,* or hundred. Each härad had a regular assembly, or *ting,* and an elected leader. Several härads in turn formed a *landskap,* or province, which likewise had its assembly, its code of laws, and its *lagman,* or "law man." Residence in a given landskap conferred "citizenship" on an individual, and anyone from beyond the province was considered a "foreigner." When the various provinces were finally united under a single king, the latter became both the political and spiritual leader of the entire realm. Although the king himself was elected, between him and the people stood the "law man" of each province as the highest elected representative from each component part of the kingdom.

So strong was the tradition of local self-government that a king was king in name only until he formally acknowledged his obligations to the individual provinces. As a result, there came into being a highly significant political ceremony with a carefully prescribed geographic basis—the *eriksgata,* or "street of the all-powerful king." No monarch of a united Sweden was considered legally elected until he had ridden his eriksgata, a route which took him, in clockwise sequence, to all the provinces of the realm. While on this journey the king was to be accompanied by the leading men of each of the respective provinces while he was in their territory. On reaching the border of the next province, he was met by a new party of notables and given hostages and pledges of peace. In each province the king had the right to collect a homage fee and could grant pardon to three criminals, providing they had not been convicted of murder. At the assembly site in each province, the king was required to pledge his faithfulness to his subjects, promise them peace, and swear not to infringe on their local laws. This done, the provincial law man would solemnly proclaim him king. Even after

Sweden was Christianized, the church would not confirm the king's coronation until all of the provincial homage ceremonies had first been carried out in the prescribed manner.

The traditional route of the medieval eriksgata led from Uppsala southward to Enköping and across the islands of the Mälaren to Strängnäs. There the king was met by the "South Men" and conducted to the ting site at Nyköping, whence he was accompanied to the wooded slopes of Kolmården. The East Goths then escorted him to their ting site at Linköping and on to the slope of Holaveden, overlooking the shore of Lake Vättern. Here the men of Småland were on hand to accompany the king to Jönköping and beyond to the bank of the little river Junabäck. On the opposite bank the West Goths were waiting to escort the king to their ting site at Skara, whence the route turned northeastward to Tiveden. Amidst these forested heights the men of Närke rendezvoused with the king, riding on to Örebro and the Arboga river, where the royal entourage was given over to the "West Men." They in turn rode with the king through Västerås to the river Sagån, whence the return to Uppsala was made in the company of the men of Uppland.

DEVELOPMENT OF THE CAPITAL
AND CORE OF SWEDEN

The choice of Uppsala as the first capital of a united Sweden was a natural one, for it had been paganism's greatest temple-site and consequently, the residence of the highest spiritual leader, the king. With the introduction of Christianity its prominence was further enhanced when it was made the archepiscopal see of Sweden in 1164. Yet, its access to the sea—all important to commercial growth—was rapidly deteriorating due to the isostatic rise of the land (following glaciation). Thus, Sweden's first real trading center arose at Birka, on a small island in Mälaren. But even Birka's access became increasingly difficult, and in the mid-thirteenth century a new settlement was established on some small islands (Swedish, *holmar*) at the entrance to the Mälaren. The fact that these islands could be linked to the adjacent mainland with log booms (Swedish *stok-kar*) and chains provided the settlement not only with its name, Stockholm, but also with its strategic significance as the guardian of the sea approaches to Sweden's core area.

The founding of Stockholm as a defensive point and center of commerce occurred at a time when Swedish contacts with other countries were expanding rapidly. More than four centuries earlier, residents of Roslagen (literally, "the district of the *Ros*," pronounced Roos) north of Stockholm had begun voyages of exploration and trade eastward across the Baltic, into the Gulf of Finland and up the river systems of what they called "Greater Sweden." To these intrepid Vikings can be traced the Finnish name for Sweden (*Ruotsi*), the origins and name of the Russian state, and the earliest Scandinavian contacts with the Moslem lands adjoining the Black and Caspian Seas. A century before Stockholm's founding, Roslagen served as a springboard for King Erik IX, later patron saint of Sweden, to launch his first crusade against Finland. Erik ultimately annexed that country not only to the realm of Latin Christendom, but also to the political dominions of Sweden. With the development of trade under the Hanseatic League, Stockholm became the primary export port for the copper and iron ore of Bergslagen (literally, "the mining district") to the northwest. However, the influence of the Hansa on the economic and social life of the Swedish core became so pronounced that a German, Albrecht of Mecklenburg, acceded to the throne in 1363. Resentful of this foreign domination, but unable to throw it off without outside assistance, the Swedes deposed him in 1388 and elected Margrethe, Queen of Denmark-Norway, as their sovereign. For nearly a century and a half to follow, the fortunes of Sweden were to be guided from Copenhagen rather than from Stockholm.

Geography had nonetheless cast the die. Stockholm was to remain the political nerve-center of Sweden, and Bergslagen was to remain the country's economic core. Because the mines of Bergslagen had come to depend on the Hansa for a market, the miners of the district were among the first to rise up against the Danes. Unrest spread until all parts of the country were involved. When the first Swedish *Riksdag,* or national assembly, was convened at Arboga in 1435, it elected a Bergslagen peasant leader, Engelbrekt Engelbrektsson, as regent. Thoughts of liberation were premature, however, and the church unpatriotically sided with the Danes in the continuing struggle. Finally, in an effort to crush Swedish resistance once and for all, Christian II landed in Stockholm in 1520 and summarily had all leaders of the nationalist movement executed in the public square. But instead of snuffing out the rebellion, the Stockholm massacre rekindled the flame even more brightly. Under the leadership of a young nobleman named Gustavus Vasa, a peasant army, recruited chiefly from Bergslagen, decisively defeated the Danes, and in 1523 an independent Sweden gratefully named him king.

The liberation of Sweden from Denmark was quickly followed by the country's liberation from Rome. Not only did the church own four times as much land as the crown did, but, as noted earlier, its attitude toward Swedish independence had also been essentially negative. The Reformation thus provided a vital instrument for furthering the nationalist cause, both financially and ideologically. Within another decade (1537), Gustavus Vasa had nationalized all foreign commercial interests, smashed the monopoly of the Hansa, and begun his country's ascendancy as the greatest power in the Baltic.

SWEDEN AS A GREAT POWER

Denmark, of course, spared no effort to thwart Swedish ambitions, and in the centuries which followed it repeatedly allied itself with Poland and Russia against its Scandinavian neighbor. The coalition was largely ineffective, however, and Sweden proceeded to deal with them individually. In 1595 Estonia was annexed by Sweden, thereby giving her control over both shores of the Gulf of Finland and the major trade route to Russia. In 1617 Gustavus

Adolphus, grandson of Gustavus Vasa, shut Russia out of the Baltic entirely by annexing Karelia and Ingermanland (around present-day Leningrad). By 1629 he had wrested control of Livonia from Poland and had incorporated Kurland into the Swedish sphere of influence. The following year he joined battle with the German Protestants against the Austrians, no doubt motivated as much by his concern over the maritime ambitions of the Hapsburgs as he was by the fate of his brothers in faith. Although Gustavus Adolphus lost his life at Lützen in 1632, by the Treaty of Westphalia (1648) Sweden further strengthened her geopolitical position by acquiring a toehold in Pomerania and the Bishopric of Bremen. In the process she not only managed to outflank Denmark, but she also established an alliance with France which was to have lasting effects. When Denmark panicked into attacking Sweden in 1643, she was quickly beaten down and in 1645 had to give up the islands of Ösel and Gotland in the Baltic as well as Jämtland and Härjedalen to the north and part of Halland province on the Swedish mainland. A decade later, the success of Swedish armies in Poland prompted the Danes to renew the struggle, but this time Denmark itself was invaded, and Swedish troops crossed the ice between the islands to capture the Danish navy and lay siege to Copenhagen. In 1660 the last Danish provinces on the Swedish mainland were surrendered, thereby allowing Sweden to share control of the access route to the Baltic, which had now become virtually a Swedish lake.

Although Sweden emerged as a circum-marine state in the late 17th century, her position in the long run was untenable, for her colonies on the periphery were too vulnerable and the resources of the mother country were inadequate to maintain them. On the mainland of Europe she had only one friend, France, who saw in Sweden an ally for furthering her own grand design. Sweden's involvement in the Dutch War (1672-1679) was at the instigation of the French, who at least managed to salvage at the treaty table what the Swedes had lost on the battlefield. Nevertheless, when Denmark, Poland, and Russia declared war on Sweden in 1700, the French did nothing to come to her aid. It was the military genius of Karl XII, then only 18 years of age, that crushed Denmark by a bold invasion, then decisively defeated the army of Peter the Great at Narva, and went on to rout the Poles.

With Denmark and Poland out of the war, Karl had to turn his attention back to Peter the Great, who had used the respite to rebuild his forces. It was on this venture that the high-water mark of Swedish expansion was reached. Deep in the Ukraine, where an anticipated anti-Russian uprising failed to materialize, where supplies and reinforcements failed to reach them, and where they encountered a much larger Russian force, the army of Karl XII met disaster at Poltava in July 1709. Denmark and Poland now reentered the war, accompanied by the German states of Prussia, Saxony, and Hanover. When the Great Northern War finally came to an end in 1721, Karl was dead (having been killed during an invasion of Norway in 1718) and Sweden's short-lived supremacy in the Baltic was no more. Actually, Sweden got out of the peace treaty rather well, for the status quo was reestablished with Saxony and Poland, and the territories lost to Russia, Prussia, and Hanover were "paid for" with five million thalers. On the other hand, the Danes forced the Swedes to pay 600,000 thalers in reparations for the territories which they restored to Sweden and also to give up their freedom from custom duties on the Öresund (Sound).

In the century which followed, Sweden was involved in two mismanaged wars against Russia, both at the behest of France. Finally, when France itself (under Napoleon) began to threaten Sweden's last remaining toehold in Pomerania, Sweden joined the struggle against her in league with Austria, Russia, and England. When France and Russia came to terms in the Treaty of Tilsit two years later, the former gave the latter the "go-ahead" to conquer Finland. As victorious Russian armies pushed through Finland and across the ice of the Åland islands to threaten Stockholm itself, the Danes saw a chance for revenge and joined the struggle. The resulting chaos within Sweden did not end until the king had been deposed and a new constitution had been promulgated. Thus, the victim of both her traditional "ally" and her traditional antagonists, Sweden's fortunes were at the lowest ebb since the country gained her independence from Denmark nearly three hundred years earlier.

In 1810, motivated by the desire to reestablish good relations with Napoleon, the Swedish Riksdag invited one of his lieutenants, Marshal Bernadotte, to become Crown Prince and heir to the Swedish throne. Napoleon was unable to resist this compliment, and Bernadotte accepted the position under the name of Karl Johan. At the same time, Napoleon induced Sweden to declare war on England—a situation which put Sweden and Denmark on the same side for the first time in their history.

But Bernadotte soon proved that he had a mind of his own. He realized that Sweden had more to gain *from* Denmark than *with* her, so early in 1812 he concluded a treaty with Russia against France. In return for his promise to make a diversion against the French in northern Germany, Russia promised to allow him to annex Norway from Denmark. To this end, he concluded peace with England the following June when Napoleon launched his disastrous invasion of Russia and joined battle against his former commander at Leipzig in October 1813. Thus, when Bernadotte acceded to the throne in 1818, it was as the king of a dual monarchy of Sweden-Norway.

The Napoleonic Wars proved at least two things as far as Sweden was concerned—first, that the age-old rivalry with Denmark was as strong as ever, and second, that other powers were now exploiting this rivalry for their own interests. However reluctant they were to admit it, the Swedes had come to realize that Great Power status was a thing of the past. Neither the size nor the resources of their land could measure up to the ambition and will of their leaders. Each grudging concession made to the Norwegians during the next 90 years was as indicative of that fact as it was inevitable. Finally, when the Norwegian parliament voted to dissolve the union in 1905, reason made its ultimate triumph over emotion and the two countries parted in peace.

THE POLITICAL AND ECONOMIC DEVELOPMENT
OF MODERN SWEDEN

During this period of agonizing reassessment, the foundations of Swedish democracy were strengthened and, despite the massive emigration which took place—and no doubt because of it as well —the economy began to develop rapidly. In 1866 the Riksdag was reconstructed as a bicameral body, with the members of the second chamber being elected by direct popular vote. Thus, it is to this date that true parliamentary government and the party system in Sweden may be traced. In all, five political parties came into being, each representing distinct economic classes. The Conservative party spoke for the government functionaries, businessmen, and wealthy landowners, while the Agrarian party became the instrument of the small farmers. The Liberals, or People's party, attracted support from amongst industrialists, intellectuals, and protagonists of various temperance movements. The Social Democrats had their greatest appeal among industrial workers, in academic circles, and in the more radical elements of the state employees. Inevitably, the Communists attracted a following among a small but vociferous group of longshoremen, lumberjacks, and Lappland miners. The last time that the Conservatives formed the government of Sweden was in 1930, and the Liberals constituted their last government in 1932. The Social Democrats came to power during the depths of the world depression and have remained the guiding force in Swedish political life ever since. An Agrarian government held power briefly during the summer of 1936 and was replaced by a Social Democrat-Agrarian coalition which stayed in office until the outbreak of World War II. Then, in the interest of national unity, an all-party coalition was created which persisted until the conflict was over. Since 1945 the Social Democrats have again dominated the government, though not since 1940 have they held an absolute majority in the Second Chamber. It is interesting that with each new election their number of mandates decreases further—ironic evidence that the welfare-state which they fashioned has been so successful that it has bred a new class of "conservatives."

THE SPECIAL ROLE OF NORRLAND
IN SWEDEN'S ECONOMY AND DEFENSE

The upswing in the Swedish economy which began in the latter half of the nineteenth century can largely be traced to the building of railways, the rise of industry, and the internal colonization of Norrland, the vast northern frontier region. Started in 1856, the Swedish railway system was conceived from the first as an integrated national network with trunk lines radiating from Stockholm to Göteborg, the west coast port, to Malmö, the regional capital of the south, and northward into Norrland. So as not to compete with existing waterways—indeed, to provide access to areas not accessible by water—the trunk lines were purposely routed away from the lakes of central Sweden and from the coasts of the country. (To be sure, feeder lines were constructed later, often by private companies, between the established, water-oriented towns and the state-owned arterial system.) Such a policy had the effect of creating a whole series of new "station towns" and a host of strategic junction points. Typical of the latter is Hallsberg, south of Örebro in central Sweden, where the main north-south and east-west lines intersect.

Although the rail network of south and central Sweden was rapidly filled in, both by the state-owned trunk lines and by the privately-owned connecting lines, in sparsely populated Norrland the arterial line paralleling the coast long remained the only tentacle reaching into this remote region. To remedy this situation and improve the region's defensibility, a second "Inland Railway" was constructed along the foothill zone of the interior. Completed in 1936, it remains an alternate route to the north which has greater potential strategic significance than actual economic importance.

The industrial development of Sweden, though chiefly concentrated in the south and center of the country, likewise involved Norrland in large degree. The rising demand for saw timber in western Europe gave the heretofore worthless stands of spruce and pine in northern Sweden a new and unexpected value. Sawmill towns sprang up at the river mouths all along the Bothnian coast. The discovery of ways to make paper from wood pulp spurred the economy of Norrland still further, and the region rapidly became the source of Sweden's most valuable exports.

Norrland made other major contributions to the industrial growth of Sweden, too. Historically, Bergslagen, on the southern margin of the region, had always been the country's mineral treasure-house. However, further mineralogical exploration uncovered a complex series of ores along the Skellefte river in the far north—ores that contained a variety of metallic elements, including lead, zinc, copper, gold, and silver. Farther north in Lappland, the existence of literally mountains of high-grade iron ore had been known for centuries, but their exploitation had to await the arrival of an inexpensive means of mass transport. The first main-line electric railway in Scandinavia was that which connected the mines at Kiruna and Gällivare with the shipping ports at Luleå (on the Gulf of Bothnia) and Narvik (on a fjord having access to the Atlantic), and even today it remains the railway which carried the heaviest volume of freight traffic in all of Northern Europe.

Norrland has become a major exporter not only of timber and minerals, but also of electric power. Eighty percent of Sweden's hydroelectric potential is found within the region, though a like proportion of the country's demand for energy is located in the center and south. Thus, the Swedes have been obliged to construct some of the longest and highest-tension transmission lines in the world in order to connect the "supply" with the "demand." A prime example is the 580-mile line which carries 380,000 volts from a generating station near Gällivare to Hallsberg in central Sweden.

The dynamic role which Norrland has played in the development of the Swedish economy has led Swedish strategists to reevaluate both the region's location and its importance in terms of the national defense. Two facts, in particular, have emerged: first, that Norrland's common land frontier with Finland in the northeast is demarcated essentially along rivers and is not in itself defensible;

and second, that any military threat to Sweden by land most likely would come from the east. Prompted by these considerations, the Swedes undertook the construction of a secret chain of fortifications in the zone between the boundary rivers and the Kiruna railway, extending from the Gulf of Bothnia on the south to the mountains on the Norwegian frontier in the north. Anchored on the railway junction point of Boden, the so-called "Boden Line" typifies an era in military thinking now largely eclipsed by advances in weapons technology.

NEUTRALITY: THE "MIDDLE WAY" IN SWEDISH FOREIGN POLICY

On the international scene Sweden has followed a course during the twentieth century which can best be called fortuitous. At the outbreak of World War I, the three Scandinavian states convened a conference at Malmö to declare their neutrality. Though the merchant fleets of all three suffered losses during the ensuing struggle, the neutrality of none of them was seriously compromised by the belligerents. After the war Sweden gave active support to the League of Nations, but as that body proved itself increasingly ineffectual, Sweden gradually moved back to its line of strict neutrality. The rise of Nazi Germany prompted Sweden to begin building up its defenses in 1936, and the next year an attempt was made to weld the Scandinavian countries into a mutual defense bloc (the so-called "Oslo States"). When World War II broke out, however, Sweden was little better prepared than either Denmark or Norway, and once again the three Scandinavian states declared their neutrality.

Almost immediately Sweden's neutrality was put to the test, for the Russian attack on Finland in the winter of 1939-1940 aroused great public concern and sympathy. Although the government officially adopted a "hands off" policy, it did not prevent the sending of volunteers and supplies to the fighting front. Widespread relief programs were also set in motion, but when the English requested permission to send troops through Sweden to Finland, they were refused. Toward the end of the war, Sweden served as the mediator between the two belligerents.

The ink was hardly dry on the Finno-Russian armistice when Nazi Germany invaded and occupied Denmark and Norway. That the same fate did not befall Sweden was most likely due to the fact that Russia advised the German high command against such a move. Certainly Swedish defenses at that juncture would have been no match for the Nazi blitzkrieg. German demands on Sweden to permit the movement of military trains through the country to Norway were refused as long as there seemed to be any hope for the Norwegian resistance forces. Once hostilities ceased, however, the Swedish government felt she must acquiesce in order to avoid being involved in a hopeless war of her own. The last major concession made to the Germans occurred in June 1941 when an entire Nazi division was transferred across Sweden to northern Finland in preparation for Hitler's attack on the Soviet Union. Throughout the war, however, the strong reaction of public opinion revealed the great strain of conscience under which the Swedes were forced to live.

Sweden's good fortune in being spared the oppression of war and occupation ultimately worked to the advantage of many Europeans, including her Scandinavian neighbors. About 50,000 Norwegians and some 18,000 Danes (including virtually the entire Jewish colony) found refuge in Sweden during the war, as well as many thousands from the Baltic states. The Swedish king personally interceded in behalf of the Hungarian Jews, and the Swedish legation in Budapest issued thousands of emergency passports to persecuted Jews of other nationalities. In the spring of 1945, Count Folke Bernadotte secured the release of Danes and Norwegians in Nazi concentration camps and later of the other nationalities as well. In the immediate postwar period Sweden provided extensive relief to many European countries in the form of food, clothing, and prefabricated housing. More recently, Sweden's active support of the United Nations has extended her humanitarian and peace-keeping activities to areas as far afield as Palestine, the Congo, and

Cyprus. And, in the pursuit of these objectives, two distinguished Swedish statesmen, Count Bernadotte and the Secretary-General of the United Nations, Dag Hammarskjöld, have given their lives.

In the post-World War II era, Sweden has chosen to continue playing the role of a neutral. To be sure, few Swedes believe that simply by declaring themselves neutral in a contest between adjacent Great Powers their independence or survival will be guaranteed; that illusion was shattered by the German occupation of Denmark and Norway during World War II. It is obvious that the Great Powers will violate a country's neutrality wherever and whenever it serves their interests to do so. Thus, Sweden has resolved that the Great Powers must be taught respect for her neutrality by building and maintaining the strongest defenses of which the country is capable. Unavoidably this has meant the diversion of vast amounts of time, effort, and money to unproductive and often questionable ends. In the process Sweden has built the "Boden Line" to guard the northern land approaches to the Scandinavian Peninsula, trained and equipped a highly mobile and efficient Home Guard, created a modern tactical air force and navy complete with underground installations, and developed the most elaborate civil defense program of any country in the world. How much of a deterrent this presents to any potential violator of Swedish neutrality becomes problematical, especially when jet bombers stand poised 10 minutes away and missiles are closer still in point of time.

Fundamental to the entire issue of Swedish neutrality is the question of which Great Power constitutes the principal threat. Certainly, the NATO powers (including Denmark, Norway, and Iceland) pose no menace to Sweden, nor does Sweden present any threat to them. Obviously the challenge comes from the Soviet Union and the Warsaw Pact countries; and to them, Sweden constitutes a menace only if allied with the West. If Sweden were attacked from the east, it is unlikely that NATO would sit idly by; its forces would be committed almost as surely as if Sweden herself were a member of the alliance. Thus, for whatever it is worth, Sweden can count on support from the West without actually making herself a party to NATO, while at the same time allaying the fears of the Warsaw Pact bloc. As long as these fears are not heightened, there is little likelihood that counter-moves will be made against Finland, whose neutrality is, perforce, oriented more eastward than westward. In effect, Sweden's armed neutrality has checkmated the "Cold War" in Norden; consequently, any change in this basic policy could only upset the power balance in all of Northern Europe.

A major question regarding Swedish nonalignment still remains to be answered, however. Can Sweden continue to pursue an independent course politically and militarily if she is welded ever more closely into a western European economic union? Already a member of EFTA, Sweden regards her eventual association with an enlarged "Common Market" as both necessary and desirable. Yet, while such association may be essential to the country's continued economic growth, it could also mean—at least in East European eyes—closer identification with the political policies being advanced by such countries as de Gaullist France and a remilitarized West Germany. Like other neutralist members of EFTA (Switzerland, Austria, and Finland), Sweden is anxious to avoid even the appearance of identification with such policies as these countries have enunciated. As a state with both the technological and financial resources to become an atomic power in its own right, Sweden has unswervingly opposed the proliferation of nuclear weapons and renounced any intention to make or acquire them. Accordingly, she views de Gaulle's *force de frappe* and the multilateral nuclear force (MLF) being pushed by West Germany as moves more likely to increase world tensions than to allay them. As long as Sweden remains economically and politically somewhat aloof from the major West European powers, she can openly and dispassionately espouse such views. But, once Sweden is drawn firmly into the economic orbits of these countries, what room for independent political manuever will remain for her? How much of Sweden's self-expression as a neutral is due to the fact that she is not deeply involved economically with either of the primary nuclear powers?

And how much of this freedom of self-expression will be lost if she becomes economically enmeshed with the aspiring second-order atomic powers? Certainly, if history holds any lesson, it is that political independence varies inversely with economic dependence. How to chart a course which will permit Sweden to play an active role in the continuing economic integration of western Europe and yet not compromise her political independence as a neutral promises to pose the greatest challenge to the country's policy-makers in the months and years that lie ahead.

Finland: Eastern Buffer

A s an independent sovereign state, Finland has yet to complete her first half century. Yet, in that time she has fought four wars. The first was a civil war at the birth of the republic; the other three have been wars with the Soviet Union, primarily over the issue of Karelia and the eastern borderlands. Just as Schleswig provided a perennial source of irritation on Norden's southern land frontier, Karelia has proved a chronic trouble-spot on the region's eastern land approaches.

Although the history of the Finnish Republic is short, the history of armed conflict on Finnish soil is long. For over eight centuries the territory of Finland has been a battleground between "west" and "east," between Swede and Russian. During six of those centuries the Swedish tide flowed ever eastward, only to ebb westward again since the time of Peter the Great. The emergence of an independent Finland in 1917 finally interposed a buffer between the age-old antagonists, but it did not put an end to the conflicts, as we have seen.

THE EMERGENCE OF NATIONALISM AND THE FINNISH STATE

It was not until the early decades of the nineteenth century, after the country had been joined to the Russian Empire as a Grand Duchy, that a vocal Finnish nationalism began to manifest itself. Throughout the entire period of Swedish domination, every effort to promote a Finnish consciousness was discouraged. Indeed, it was only with great reluctance that the Swedish authorities permitted the translation of the New Testament into the Finnish language in 1548. This event not only gave the Finnish language its first literary expression, but it also established the dialect of the Turku district as the national norm.

The Russians, on the other hand, sought to encourage Finnish nationalism as a means of weakening Swedish control over the country. As early as 1742 the Empress Elizabeth exhorted the Finns to break away from Sweden and set up their own separate state. In 1812, three years after Russian arms had wrested the country away from Sweden, the capital was moved from Turku, a center of strong Swedish loyalties, to Helsinki, a city which was both geographically and ideologically more aloof from the Swedes, and which, incidentally, could be kept under surveillance from St. Petersburg more easily. In 1831 the Finnish Literary Society was founded, and four years later the crowning work of Finnish nationalism, the *Kalevala,* was first published. Though nonpolitical in spirit and content, the *Kalevala* embodies the heroic legends of Finnish mythology. Few literary works have acted as a more effective catalyst in stimulating national pride and consciousness among a people than has the *Kalevala* among the Finns, for it has ever since served as a wellspring of inspiration for artists, writers, and composers. However, it is interesting to note that the Finnish language was not granted official status until 1863, when, under the direction of the liberal Czar Alexander II, it took its place beside Swedish in the offices of administration and the courts of justice.

To be sure, the Russians continued to encourage Finnish nationalism only as long as it served their interests to do so. In 1898, under Czar Nicolas II, an intensive Russification campaign began. Not only was Russian made the administrative language of the country, but the Finnish constitution was also suspended and the secret police were given free rein to stamp out any and all resistance. The confusion resulting from the Russo-Japanese War of 1904-1905 gave the Finns an opportunity to reinstitute a revised constitution which, among other things, created a unicameral parliament and gave women the right to vote. Once the crisis in the Far East was over, however, the Russians resumed their pan-Slavic campaign against the country, with the Finns powerless but to respond with passive resistance.

During World War I the Finnish parliament was dominated by the Social Democratic party (founded in 1897). Because it represented the interests of the working class, it looked with favor on the Bolshevik revolution which overthrew the Czar. Seizing this moment of chaos in which to act, the Finnish parliament declared the country's independence from Russia on December 6, 1917. To be free of Russian domination was something on which all Finnish political parties could agree; but which form of government the new state should adopt was an issue on which there was sharp division. Late in January 1918, the Red Guard, a workers' militia which had been created to maintain peace during the disorders of 1905, sought to establish a Socialist Workers' Republic through a *coup d'état.* The White Guard, a countermovement initiated by the non-Socialist parties, immediately responded with force of arms, and from January until May of 1918 the country was engaged in a fierce civil war. The Reds could count on no support from their "brothers in arms" in Russia; the Whites, in turn, could find no assistance forthcoming from the neutral Swedes, so they turned to Germany with a call for help. The tide of battle had already turned in favor of the Whites under General Mannerheim when men and material began flowing in from Germany, but their arrival clinched the victory and brought the struggle to an end. Twenty-four thousand persons had been killed, and the abyss of bitterness and distrust which divided the Finns of the working class from those of the middle and upper classes was now deeper than it had ever been before.

The rump parliament which was convened at the termination of hostilities refused to seat the Social Democratic members and, acting without them, voted to establish a monarchy. In October 1918 the same body elected the brother-in-law of Germany's Kaiser Wilhelm to be the King of Finland. Within a month, however, Germany had been defeated on the western front and the Kaiser himself was without a throne. Thus, the Allied victory had the double-barreled effect of obliging Finland to assume a republican form of government (with General Mannerheim being appointed Regent) and of precluding the country's emergence as a vassal state of Germany. On July 17, 1919, the Form of Government Act was promulgated, officially creating the Republic of Finland, and in the same year a new parliament and the country's first president were elected.

Meanwhile, the chaos which continued to prevail in Russia due to the civil war and the Allied intervention encouraged Finland to press her claims for Karelia. War broke out between the two countries in June 1919, and, after much heavy fighting, was brought to an end by the Treaty of Dorpat in October 1920. Russia was obliged to recognize that the Finnish Republic's boundaries should be those which prevailed when Finland was a Grand Duchy, thereby renouncing her claim to the city of Viipuri (Vyborg) and the Karelian Isthmus. In addition, Russia was forced to cede a strip of territory in the far north giving Finland access to the ice-free Arctic coast and the port of Petsamo (Pechenga).

At the same time, Sweden voiced her claim to the Åland Islands, the strategically located archipelago at the entrance to the Gulf of Bothnia. Sweden argued that these islands were Swedish territory lost to the Russians in 1809, while the Finns contended that the archipelago had been part of the Finnish realm since the Middle Ages. The islanders themselves, almost all of whom were Swedish-speaking, sought to have the area reunited with Sweden. The dispute was submitted to a League of Nations commission which finally ruled in favor of Finland. Significantly, the ruling was based on a climatic factor, namely that during the winter the archipelago is joined to the Finnish mainland by a traversable ice field and thus should be considered part of Finland. The commission recommended that the islands should be demilitarized and should be granted a substantial measure of autonomy. As a result, Ålanders are exempt from Finnish military service, but must serve as coast-wise pilots and lighthouse keepers. Swedish is recognized as the islands' official tongue, and Finnish-speaking persons are discouraged from emigrating to the archipelago.

THE INTERNAL STRUGGLE: LEFT VS. RIGHT

Although Finland's international disputes were quickly settled, her internal political problems admitted of no easy solution. The struggle between left and right which had already torn the country by civil war continued as the underlying theme of domestic relations during the following decades. Despite the fact that the Social Democratic party had been banned from the parliament which promulgated the Form of Government Act, it reemerged as the country's strongest political party in the elections of 1919, winning 80 of the 200 seats in parliament. Later the same year, however, the "left wing" split off from the party and established itself as the Finnish Communist party. Although it patterned itself after the Communist party of the Soviet Union, it never became associated with the Comintern. This split in the "left" was welcomed by the rightists, who nevertheless considered both the Social Democrats and the Communists as instruments of the devil, differing only in degree.

When the Communists appeared on the ballot in the elections of 1922, they elected 27 members to parliament and thereby reduced Social Democratic representation by the same number. In the election of 1924 they succeeded in taking only 18 seats, while the Social Democrats pushed their total to 60. Three years later the Social Democrats returned the same number of members, while the Communists increased their mandate to 20. However, the greatest gains in the 1927 election were scored by the Agrarians, who two years later edged out the Social Democrats as the country's strongest single party. The only other party that gained in 1929 was the Communist, which increased its mandate to 23. Never before had the parties of the left commanded so great a number of seats in the Finnish parliament.

The rightists could no longer conceal their mounting fear. Using force to break up a Communist rally in the central Finnish town of Lapua, they touched off a nationwide series of riots which culminated in a march on Helsinki. There, by threatening to continue and even increase their violence, they blackmailed the Finnish parliament into outlawing the Communist party and calling new elections for the following year.

In the 1930 elections, with the Communists either not voting or "going underground," the Conservative party surged dramatically ahead. Nonetheless, those Communists who did vote, cast their ballots in favor of the Social Democrats, thereby reestablishing that party as the country's strongest single political faction.

When the election of 1933 was held, it was the right that was split, with a new fascistic party known as the IKL edging ahead of the Conservatives. The left rallied under the Social Democratic banner and increased its mandate significantly. In 1936 the IKL lost ground as many rightists returned to the traditional Conservative fold. The left continued to gain, however, with the Social Democrats reaching a high of 83 seats, one more than the combined Social Democratic-Communist mandate in 1929. By 1939 the right had slipped yet farther into its more traditional alignment, with the IKL copping fewer than one-third as many seats as the Conservatives. The left, however, further increased its strength, winning a total of 85 seats, the largest number ever held by a single party in the Finnish parliament.

WAR AND PEACE WITH RUSSIA

During the summer of 1939, as ominous storm clouds gathered over Europe, Finnish attention was shifted abruptly to the international arena. The Soviet Union requested that Finland cede to it some small islands guarding the approaches to the city of Leningrad. Marshal Mannerheim recommended compliance with the Soviet request, but the government, without consulting Parliament, summarily refused. In October of the same year, a few weeks after the Nazi war machine started rolling eastward across Poland, the Soviets presented Finland with new and more extensive demands, namely the lease of the Hanko Peninsula (which controls the northern side of the entrance to the Gulf of Finland) and the cession of part of the Karelian Isthmus (where the Finnish boundary lay only a dozen miles from Leningrad). In return the Soviets offered to make a boundary adjustment in favor of Finland farther north along the Karelian frontier. The Finns replied with a series of counterproposals which the Soviets found completely unacceptable, and on November 30 Soviet aircraft bombed Helsinki.

Through the first six weeks of the ensuing struggle, Marshal Mannerheim's small army put up an heroic resistance, fighting in the −40° F. cold of one of the severest winters of this century. By mid-January, when Soviet forces were reorganized to take the offensive, lakes, swamps, and even the Gulf of Finland itself were solidly frozen over. Seizing the strategic opportunity presented by the climate, Soviet tanks crossed the Gulf of Finland and attacked the Finnish lines from the rear. The hopelessness of the Finnish position was soon apparent, and early in March the government was obliged to sign a peace treaty with the Soviet Union.

That the so-called "Winter War" was one of limited Soviet objectives rather than an all-out attempt to subjugate Finland is clear from the terms of the treaty, all of which related directly to the improvement of the defensive position of the U.S.S.R. In addition to the cession of the small islands on the approaches to Leningrad, the treaty called for the cession of the entire Karelian Isthmus, including Viipuri, Finland's third largest city; the lease of the Hanko Peninsula; and the cession of a northern border district known as Kuusamo-Salla. While the first three changes contributed to the security of the Soviet Union's second largest city, the latter had as its objective the removal of the "threat" posed to the Murmansk railway at a point where the Finnish boundary most closely approached this vital communications link.

Following the cessation of hostilities, Finland's most immediate domestic problem was the relocation of some 400,000 refugees from the ceded areas. On the international scene, one of her first moves was to propose—over Soviet protests—a defensive alliance with

Sweden and Norway. Within a month, however, both Denmark and Norway had been occupied by Nazi Germany and Sweden's neutrality was facing its most critical test. Beginning in September, 1940, the Nazis put pressure on Sweden and Finland to permit troop movements to and from North Norway across the national territories of both states. By the following summer, when Hitler unleashed his blitzkrieg against the Soviet Union, a full German division had been transferred to northern Finland for a drive against the Murmansk railway.

Three days after the Nazis opened their offensive on the eastern front, Finland joined the war against the Soviet Union. In what everyone believed would be a quick victory, the Finns hoped to regain the territories lost in the preceding year. Indeed, within three months the former boundary had been regained, and thousands of Karelians began streaming back to their farmsteads. But as the struggle wore through 1942, it became increasingly clear that there would be no quick victory, and more and more Finns called for their country's withdrawal from the war. In the spring of 1943 an American offer of mediation was rejected, but after a stern warning from the United States in February, 1944, the Finns agreed to open peace talks with the Soviets. The terms offered, namely a return to the 1940 boundaries and the payment of an indemnity, seemed unduly harsh, and the Finns elected to fight on. The mounting of a new and more powerful Soviet offensive in the summer of 1944 convinced all but a few die-hards of the hopelessness of the situation, and on September 4, 1944, the Finnish government, with Marshal Mannerheim as its president, signed a separate peace treaty with the Soviet Union. The terms of the armistice, announced two weeks later, included cession of the Karelian Isthmus and the Kuusamo-Salla district as before. However, rather than leasing the Hanko Peninsula, the Soviets demanded a 50-year lease on the Porkkala Peninsula, a dozen miles west of Helsinki and directly opposite the Estonian capital of Tallinn. In addition, they demanded the cession of the Petsamo area in the far north, thereby removing the Finnish "threat" to Murmansk and reestablishing a common frontier with Norway.

In addition to the territorial changes Finland assumed the responsibility of paying reparations in the amount of $300,000,000 over a six-year period and the immediate evacuation of all German troops within the country. The latter was more difficult than could have been imagined, for the Nazis refused to acquiesce to Finland's withdrawal from the struggle. As they retreated across Lappland in the face of the Red Army they completely scorched the countryside, burning all habitations and blowing up all communications lines. It was not until April, 1945, that the last of the 200,000 German troops stationed in the country had been either killed, captured, or driven across the borders into Sweden and Norway.

The Peace Treaty signed in Paris on February 10, 1947, between Finland and the Allies restated the principal clauses of the armistice. The territories had already been transferred and the reparations payments were being made right on schedule. Nevertheless, later that year, when Finland applied for membership in the United Nations, her application was vetoed by the Soviet Union. In April, 1948, at the suggestion of the Soviet Union, the two countries signed a 10-year Agreement of Friendship, Cooperation, and Mutual Assistance, which, together with the armistice of 1944 and the peace treaty of 1947, has become the cornerstone of postwar Finnish policy. The motivation for the agreement is clearly discernible in the first and fourth articles, which commit Finland to repel any attack "on the part of Germany or any State allied with the latter" against Finland "or the Soviet Union across the territory of Finland" and to refrain from concluding any alliance or joining any coalition "directed against the other party." Then, as a gesture of good will toward Finland, the Soviet Union wrote off half of the remaining reparations deliveries (reducing the total to $226,500,000) and extended the repayment period by a further two years.

In the years which followed, Finland's closest relations continued to be with her Scandinavian neighbors. Nevertheless, when the Nordic Council was established in 1953, Finland did not feel free to take part in its deliberations because the Soviet Union was suspicious of its purpose. After the death of Stalin, however, Finnish-Soviet relations took on an easier and more cordial air. In September, 1955, the Soviet Union returned the Porkkala peninsula to Finland (its strategic significance impaired by the march of weapons technology). At the same time it suggested that the Agreement on Friendship, Cooperation, and Mutual Assistance be extended for 20 years (to 1975), and Finland assented. In December of the same year Finland reapplied for admission to the United Nations and was accepted with the approval of the Soviet Union. The following summer the Finns felt emboldened enough to send representatives to the meeting of the Nordic Council, and since that date they have regularly participated in its consultations.

To be sure, most major domestic issues within Finland since the war have likewise turned on the country's relations with its eastern neighbor. Although no elections were held from 1939 to 1945, when they were resumed it was with a legalized Communist party again taking an open and active part in them, due to Soviet insistence on this point. The results of the 1945 parliamentary contest gave the Social Democrats 50 seats and the Communists and Agrarians each 49. The cabinet which was formed included two Communist ministers, the first time in Finnish history that this party had participated in formulating government policy. Attempts by the Communists to exploit their toehold in the government (chiefly with their backing in the trade unions and the police force) met with solid opposition from the other parties. In the 1948 elections Communist strength in parliament was reduced to 38 seats, and the party was given no representation in the cabinet which took office. Indeed, the basic principle of all Finnish coalition governments since that date (and they have been numerous) has been to exclude the Communists from participation at the policy-making level. After the 1948, 1951, and 1954 elections, this meant cooperation between the Social Democrats and the Agrarians, who together controlled a majority of the seats in parliament. Yet, because the exclusion of Communists from the government was about the only basic issue on which these two parties could agree, the Finnish ship of state has sailed an erratic and vacillating course, especially in the realm of economic affairs. The Social Democrats, as the traditional spokesmen of the factory workers, consistently demand low food prices—if need be, with government subsidization to the consumer. The Agrarians, on the other hand, just as consistently fight for higher prices for agricultural produce with subsidies to the farmers. The seesaw struggle between the two major Finnish parties resulted in an ineffective program of price stabilization and a rapidly worsening spiral of inflation. Illustrative of the chaotic condition in which the country found itself in 1953 was the fact that the cost of living was 10 times higher in that year than it had been in 1939, while industrial wages had increased 20 times and agricultural wages 24 times in the same period.

REPARATIONS, RESETTLEMENT, AND RECONSTRUCTION

There were other, even more fundamental, causes for Finland's postwar inflation, however. Any one of them alone could have wreaked havoc on the war-weakened economy of a poor nation of four million inhabitants; all of them together posed a seemingly insurmountable challenge to the country's survival. Indeed, any lesser people than the Finns might well have failed to meet the challenge. The problems which confronted them simultaneously were:

(1) The payment of 300 million dollars in reparations to the Soviet Union within six years (later reduced to 226.5 million dollars spread over 8 years);

(2) The resettlement of the 420,000 refugees (equivalent to one-tenth of the country's total population) from the ceded eastern territories; and

(3) The reconstruction of the war-scorched northern provinces (equivalent to one-third of its national area).

The size of the Soviet reparation demands was not only staggering in itself, but the nature of the payments and their delivery deadlines also posed serious problems. For a country which derived about 90 percent of its foreign exchange from the export of wood products, a treaty which demanded two-thirds of all reparations in the form of metal and engineering products seemed uncommonly harsh. That they should be delivered according to a strict schedule, under penalty for tardiness, further heightened the complications. Immediately the Finnish government swung into action, literally creating a metal and engineering industry overnight at a time when all of Europe was desperately short of raw materials. By careful planning, systematic organization, and efficient production, all of the ships, electric cables, and machinery were delivered on time in the amounts and quality specified.

At the peak of the operation one out of every eight Finnish workers was engaged in producing reparation goods. There is little doubt but that this prodigious feat made a profound impression on the Russians. Besides proving that the Finns fully intended to live up to their treaty obligations, it demonstrated conclusively what a free and determined nation could do. In the light of the Soviet Union's own economic development and that of its satellites, the Finnish performance must have been an extremely powerful object lesson.

The resettlement of one-tenth of the country's population, most of whom were farmers, was a second problem of almost overwhelming proportions. But this the Finns tackled with the same resolution as they had the reparations demands. By the end of 1951, the relocation had been essentially completed, with over two and a half million acres having been acquired for resettlement purposes. Although some new land was taken under cultivation, most land acquisition was effected through expropriation and voluntary sales of existing farm properties. Thanks to the careful planning and financial assistance of the central government, the absorption of the Karelian refugees into the life of the country was accomplished with a minimum of social dislocation.

Concurrent with the delivery of the reparations demands and the resettlement of the Karelian refugees was the task of rebuilding

Lappland, literally from the ground up. Due to the region's geographic isolation from the country's core area and its small pioneer-fringe population, Finnish Lappland had always suffered the same neglect by the central government as the corresponding parts of Norway and Sweden had from their governments. But the final chapters of World War II changed all that, for now a new insistence, a new urgency, presented itself. Cities and towns had to be reconstructed, roads and railways restored, bridges and communication lines replaced. Through the sunlit "nights" of the long summer days work went on at a feverish pace, and by 1950 most of the scars of war had been healed. In the process, Finland's most remote region had in effect become its most modern. Today, well-planned cities like the new Rovaniemi, regional capital of Lappland, stand as eloquent testimony not alone to the functional beauty of Finnish architecture and design, but also to the resilience and determination of the Finnish nation.

THE CONTINUING ECONOMIC CRISIS
AND ITS POLITICAL OVERTONES

Finland's success in completing the reparations payments on time, in resettling the Karelian refugees, and in rebuilding Lappland tended to obscure her relative lack of success in dealing with the problems of inflation and unemployment. Rising food prices goaded the labor unions into calling widespread and repeated strikes. These, in turn, provoked cabinet crises within the Social Democratic-Agrarian coalition, toppling one government after another. When the results of the 1958 parliamentary elections were in, only the far left and the far right could point to any substantial gains. The Communists increased their seats from 43 to 50, becoming the country's largest single political party, while the Conservatives rose from 24 to 29 seats. The Agrarians lost five seats (falling to 48) and the Social Democrats dropped three (for a total of 51). The latter party was split on its policy toward President Kekkonen and his conduct of foreign affairs, especially with the Soviet Union, so that the "mother party" (the anti-Kekkonen faction) could claim the support of only 38 members while the Social Democratic Opposition party numbered 13.

Kekkonen's invitation to the Communist party leader to form a government may be viewed as merely a formality, for no other party was willing to enter a coalition with the Communists. Instead a five-party coalition headed by a Social Democrat took office. It did not last out the year, however, for the Soviet Union's reluctance to conclude its annual trade agreement with Finland was seen as a manifestation of its displeasure with the government. The resignation of the Agrarian party ministers precipitated a collapse of the government in early December, and a new Agrarian minority cabinet was not formed until over a month later. The new government immediately addressed itself to the problems of Finnish-Russian relations and unemployment, and ten days later Kekkonen and Khrushchev met in Leningrad. This meeting paved the way for the restoration of more cordial relations between the two countries, followed by the appointment of a new Soviet ambassador and the signing of a new five-year trade agreement.

Postwar unemployment, always a seasonal phenomenon in the wood industries of Finland, was further aggravated by the Soviet reparation demands, for they left the country with sizable metal and engineering industries which, in a free market situation, could hardly be considered competitive. If they were to operate, they would have to continue to look for markets within the Soviet bloc rather than in the West, where Finland's principal markets for wood products are found. The signing of the new long-term trade agreement with the Soviet Union in mid-March 1959 could hardly have come at a more auspicious time for Finland, for nearly 100,000 workers (about 7 percent of the labor force) were unemployed. By the following summer the number of unemployed had dropped to 9,000, and in June 1960 the public unemployment register was closed entirely.

Like it or not—and many Finns, especially among the Social Democrats, did not—it seemed manifestly clear that the country's economic health in a large part depended on the maintenance of cordial relations with the Soviet Union. At the same time, because Finland's traditional markets lay in the West, exploratory talks were launched with the European Free Trade Association regarding Finland's possible membership in that group. The Soviet Union indicated that it had no objection to such a link, and in March 1961 Finland became a signatory to the EFTA-Finland Association (EFA). Eventual ties with the European Economic Community (EEC) remain problematical for Finland, not only because of the rejection of Britain (Finland's leading trade partner), but also because of possible Soviet reaction to such a move.

Finnish responsiveness to the Soviet's concern for security was vividly demonstrated late in 1961 when the U.S.S.R. called upon her small neighbor for consultations pursuant to their agreement on mutual assistance. The call came at a strategic moment, for Kekkonen was in the United States and had just received official American recognition for Finnish neutrality from President Kennedy. At the same time Denmark and Norway were severely criticized by the Soviet Union for "being drawn into the German military and political sphere," while Sweden was rebuked for letting her industries contribute to the arming of the Bundeswehr. The call for consultations and the simultaneous propaganda offensive against the Scandinavian states sent an ominous chill over all of Northern Europe. President Kekkonen journeyed to the Siberian city of Novosibirsk to see Khrushchev, and in the subsequent discussion he indicated to the Soviet leader that any military consultation between the two countries would only heighten anxiety and war psychosis within the region. The Soviet leader, having already made his point, agreed that the initiative for any such consultations would rest primarily with Finland.

The success of Kekkonen's mission further enhanced his stature as a statesman and convinced a yet larger segment of the Finnish electorate of the essential soundness of the so-called "Paasakivi-Kekkonen line" (that is, the maintenance of good relations with the Soviet Union). In the presidential election of 1962, Kekkonen was returned to office by the first ballot of the electoral college. In the subsequent parliamentary elections the parties subscribing to the Kekkonen line won an additional 13 seats. The Social Democrats were so hopelessly split that they suffered a net loss of 11 seats, all of them, however, from the pro-Kekkonen Social Democratic Opposition party. Significantly, the Communist party lost three seats, dropping to 47 compared to the now first-place Agrarians with 53. Even on the far left, Finns had apparently come to realize that cooperation with the Soviet Union need not imply national subservience to their eastern neighbor. As President Kekkonen stated in a speech delivered in Moscow late in 1962, "the policy of neutrality based on the will for peace which is observed in Finland conforms with Soviet interests," adding that "it [Finland's policy of neutrality] has a wider importance as an indication that ideological differences between states need not constitute an obstacle to the solution of the ultimate question of international relations, the question of security. . . ."

As further proof of Soviet "good will" toward Finland, an agreement was signed in late 1962 for the Finnish rehabilitation and use of the Saimaa canal. This waterway links the extensive Lake Saimaa system in eastern Finland with the city of Vyborg (former Finnish Viipuri), and before the war it carried a great volume of timber traffic down to Finland's chief export port. With the boundary changes at the end of the war, both the port and the lower half of the canal were lost to Finland, thereby materially complicating the movement of wood products from the eastern interior of the country. According to the agreement, Finland would bear the cost of putting the canal back in working order (estimated at about $50 million) and would likewise pay a modest annual rental, based on the volume of goods transported. Also included in the agreement is the leasing of the island of Ravansaari in the Gulf of Viipuri for purposes of storage and loading.

With its neutrality officially recognized by all the Great Powers, Finland is cautiously charting its course toward closer cooperation with the other Nordic states while at the same time maintaining a "diplomatically correct" policy toward the Soviet Union. The ambivalence of its neutrality was revealed in 1963 when, pursuant to an amendment of the 1947 peace treaty, the country acquired defensive missiles—half of which came from the Soviet Union and half from the United Kingdom. At the same time the Finnish president observed that the "stability of Swedish foreign policy" (that is, neutrality) was basic to all of Norden—a reminder to his Scandinavian neighbors that a certain balance of power had been achieved in the North and that any change in the policy in one country would most likely be felt in all of them.

THE Republic of Iceland affords an extreme example of the dilemma in which all of Norden finds itself today. Small in population and poor in resources, Iceland is strategically situated between the two major centers of contemporary political power. For this reason, the Icelanders take small comfort in the knowledge that whatever importance they have in today's world is not primarily due to *who* they are, but rather to *where* they are.

The relative remoteness of Iceland is deceiving, for it has not spared the Icelanders from political involvement with other states in the past any more than it does today in the age of the airplane. Indeed, the very settlement of Iceland (begun in 874) was in large part a reaction to the political unification of Norway. Many Norwegian chieftains, too proud to accept the dominion of Harald the Fair-Haired, instead chose voluntary exile on this dimly known island in the western seas. Until 930, these chieftains were supreme unto themselves, serving as both the secular and religious leaders of their respective local districts. In the latter year, however, the first all-island parliament was assembled on a plain at the base of a great earthquake scarp in the southwestern interior. The convening of this parliament, or *Althing,* marked the founding of the world's oldest democracy still in existence. For more than eight and a half centuries the representatives of the Icelandic people came together for several weeks each summer to legislate and administer justice at Thingvellir (literally "Parliament Plain"). No other site is held in greater reverence by the Icelanders than this grassy bank that marks the birthplace of their commonwealth.

It was at Thingvellir in the year 1000 that the people of Iceland formally annexed themselves to the realm of Latin Christendom by adopting Christianity as the state religion. This action was not kindly received by many of the chieftains, for it obviously deprived them of their religious functions and thereby weakened their hold on the people. It marked, in fact, the beginning of a lengthy contest between church and state. Fully half a century passed before the Church emerged triumphant, with the Bishop of Skálholt becoming the spiritual leader of the country in 1056. Sectional pressures from the north, however, forced the naming of a second bishop at Hólar in 1106.

In the course of time, many of the chieftainships passed by inheritance or sale into the hands of a few powerful families. In the sagas we find recorded in intimate detail much of the intrigue and feuding which were typical of the times. Coupled with this internal political disorder was the growing realization that the island's economic resources, especially of wood, were sorely limited. For these reasons, the various warring factions sought the support of the King of Norway, who was only too happy to take full advantage of the situation. Finally in 1262, after lengthy negotiations, the Althing voted, albeit reluctantly, to swear allegiance to the King of Norway in return for the promise of at least one shipload of timber a year!

DOMINATION BY NORWAY AND DENMARK

In the centuries which followed, the Icelanders had ample opportunity to learn that political independence diminishes in direct proportion to economic dependence. With the extinction of the Norwegian royal line in 1380, the see-saw struggle between church and state shifted from Oslo to Copenhagen, but it did not abate. Indeed, it was not until the Reformation that the Danish monarch was able to finally assert his dominance over the Church. By decreeing the establishment of the Evangelical Lutheran faith as the state church in 1536, the King greatly strengthened his personal control, but in Iceland his decree had the effect of engendering widespread nationalistic resistance. The Catholic Bishop of Skálholt in particular became a symbol of Icelandic opposition to the Danish crown—an opposition which was terminated only by the ruthless execution of the bishop in 1550.

In the years which followed, the King tightened his grip on Iceland still further. In 1602 he decreed that trade with the island was to be a royal monopoly—a privilege leased only to a handful of favored merchants in Copenhagen, Helsingör, and Malmö. Later the King realized a yet greater profit by auctioning the monopoly to the highest bidder, a practice which was to have grievous consequences for the Icelanders. Not only could the company manipulate the prices of exports and imports to its own advantage, but it could also divest itself of spoiled grain by shipping it to Iceland, where the islanders had no choice but to buy it or starve. The abuses of the trade monopoly were many, and when the Danish King became absolute monarch in 1662, even most rights of appeal were lost. Nevertheless, Danish control over Iceland was not fully effective, for the trade monopoly encouraged smuggling by nationals of other countries which Denmark was largely unable to stop. Indeed, Danish surveillance of Icelandic waters was often so lax that for a time North African pirates plundered the coasts of the island, carrying off hostages almost at will.

A turning point in Danish-Icelandic relations was not reached until 1787 when trade with the island was thrown open to all Danish merchants. Though the Icelandic statesman, Skúli Magnusson, is given credit for this accomplishment, there can be little doubt but that this "change of heart" on the part of the Danes is largely attributable to the eruption of Laki in 1783-1784. This natural disaster killed nearly three-fourths of the livestock in the country (through poisonous fall-out) and resulted in the subsequent starvation of one-fifth of the island's human inhabitants. The compassion of the Danes for their fellow subjects was so stirred that they took up a national collection for the survivors (only one-fifth of which supposedly reached those for whom it was intended) and the Danish parliament seriously debated removing the remaining populace to the Heath of Jutland, a barren region with which the Danes themselves had been unable to do anything.

Hardly had the dust settled from the Laki eruption when a violent earthquake leveled the ancient religious center of Skálholt. However, rather than rebuild the country's mother church at this inland site, it was decided to transfer the see of the bishop of southern Iceland to Reykjavík, then a tiny collection of houses numbering 200 inhabitants. In 1786 the King granted Reykjavík and five other coastal settlements the right of self-government. When the trade monopoly was relaxed the following year, the strategic location of Reykjavík allowed this southwestern settlement to profit most from the freedom of commerce. In 1801 its growth was spurred by two further events. One was the abolition by royal decree of the Althing, which had long since been reduced to little more than a debating society; in its stead a court meeting in Reykjavík was established. The other was the dissolution of the Hólar bishopric and the vesting of all ecclesiastic authority in Iceland in the Bishop of Reykjavík. Hence, from that time forward the young southwestern coastal town served as the focal point of both the island's political and religious life, as well as the nucleus of its expanding economy. Throughout the island's history, the "core area" of the country had been the Southern Lowlands, but not until the beginning of the nineteenth century did Iceland likewise possess a true "capital."

To be sure, Iceland still continued to be ruled from Copenhagen, and more explicitly, by the King himself. But in Denmark, too, there was growing discontent with the absolutism of the monarchy, and finally in 1834 the King was constrained to permit the creation of a consultative assembly. This concession paved the way for a similar body (graced by the name of *Althing*) to come into being in Iceland in 1843. The popular uprisings which swept much of Europe in 1848 likewise had their repercussions in Denmark, culminating in the King's renunciation of absolute power and the promulgation of a liberal constitution in 1849. The latter, however, took no cognizance of Iceland, though five years later a further concession was made when trade with the island was opened to all nations. It was not until the occasion of the country's millennial anniversary (1874) and a visit by the Danish monarch that Iceland received a constitution of her own and that legislative rights were restored to the Althing. In 1903 the Icelanders succeeded in having a minister named who was actually resident in Reykjavík and who could both read and write the Icelandic language; in the following year the island was granted the right of home rule. Continuing Icelandic agitation and protracted negotiations ultimately resulted in the signing of the so-called Danish-Icelandic Act of Union in 1918, a document which acknowledged Iceland as a fully independent and sovereign state in personal union with the King of Denmark. This, in turn, set the stage for drawing up a new and more satisfactory constitution in 1920. Just as important, however, was an article in the Act of Union which stipulated that either the Danish *Rigsdag* or the Icelandic *Althing* could demand the treaty's revision after December 1, 1940. If no revision had been agreed upon within three years of that date, either parliament could pass a resolution abolishing the Union by a two-thirds vote. The resolution would then be submitted to a referendum for confirmation by the people. If three-fourths of the eligible electorate took part and if three-fourths of the votes cast were in favor of abrogation, the Union would be unilaterally terminated.

Although legal machinery had been set up for the orderly eventual dissolution of the Union, the march of world events introduced some complications at the eleventh hour. On April 9, 1940, Denmark was occupied by Nazi Germany and all ties with Iceland were broken. A month later, British forces moved into Iceland, seeking both to forestall a possible Nazi seizure of this strategic island and to protect the vital sea lanes to North America. Promising to respect Iceland's sovereignty, the British indicated that they would remain only as long as the exigencies of war necessitated their presence. However, by June 1941 the hard-pressed British required their Iceland garrison for other, more urgent operations, and the United States, though not yet a belligerent, was induced to assume the responsibility for the island's defense. In so doing, it likewise bound itself to respect Iceland's "complete freedom and sovereignty" and to refrain from involving itself in the country's administration "either so long as its forces remain in Iceland or afterwards."

In October 1942 the government of the United States lent its official support to the Icelandic independence movement by declaring that the country had full legal right to disassociate itself from Denmark at any time after the end of 1943. Thus, on February 25, 1944, the Althing unanimously voted to declare the Union with Denmark abrogated. In a referendum the following May 98.6 per cent of the electorate went to the polls, and 97.3 per cent of the votes cast were in favor of abrogation. On June 16 the Althing declared the Union abolished and adopted a new constitution. The next day, despite a heavy downpour of rain, the Althing and several thousand spectators assembled at Thingvellir to proclaim the birth of the new Republic of Iceland, thus bringing to an end 682 years of foreign political domination.

KEFLAVÍK AND THE AMERICAN IMPACT

Iceland's emergence as an independent nation came at a fateful time, for less than a fortnight earlier the Normandy invasion had been launched and Hitler's *Festung Europa* was beginning to crumble. Iceland itself played a vital role in Allied logistics, for the Americans had constructed a large air base at Keflavík, some 30 miles west of Reykjavík, and a naval refueling depot at Hvalfjördhur, a like distance northeast of the capital. The presence of these installations and a handful of radar and antiaircraft batteries scattered around the north and east coasts of the island, together with upwards of 10,000 armed forces personnel and civilian contractors, had already had a marked effect on the economy and social structure of the country. The lingering unemployment of the thirties had vanished overnight, and in its place a chronic labor shortage had developed. High wages offered by American military contractors drew workers away from other employment, and Icelandic wage scales climbed rapidly in a vain attempt to meet the competition. With literally thousands of dollars being pumped into the island's economy each week but with little opportunity for meeting the burgeoning demand for goods and services, prices, too, began a runaway spiral. Desperate government efforts at wage and price control managed to slow the inflation somewhat, but failed to stop it. By the end of the war in Europe, both wages and prices in Iceland were about three times higher than they had been before the country's occupation.

In October 1946, fully a year after the cessation of hostilities in the Far East, a treaty was signed which called for the removal of U.S. forces from Keflavík and for the assumption by Iceland of the responsibility for the continued maintenance and operation of the airport. By the time that the last Americans were evacuated in April 1947, the labor force at Keflavík had been reduced to a skeleton crew of about 300 Icelanders. It is significant that, with the departure of the Americans, the Icelandic government found it necessary to resume its official unemployment census. As further cutbacks and retrenchments took place in the Icelandic economy, the number of jobless climbed steadily.

In the spring of 1949 Iceland became a signatory of the North Atlantic Treaty Organization, and as such she agreed to the reactivation of the Keflavík base in a new treaty signed with the United States in May 1951. The following summer U.S. forces once more descended onto the rainy, wind-swept and treeless lava flow that had come to constitute such a vital link in the American air-defense chain.

During the reactivation of Keflavík in 1951 no new construction took place, and by the following winter unemployment reached a postwar peak in Iceland, with nearly 700 jobless in Reykjavík alone. In 1952, however, contracts for over $1.5 million were let for new construction, and hirings began to pick up. In 1953 nearly $12 million was poured into new construction, and by the autumn of that year over 3000 Icelanders—about 5 percent of the total labor force —were employed at the base. Once again the Icelandic government saw fit to discontinue its census of unemployment.

Although United States expenditures for construction tapered off somewhat in subsequent years, the annual rate of investment at Keflavík continued in excess of $9 million. Thus, in the period from July 1951 to June 1956 the United States spent a total of more than $51 million at the airport, or about $360 for every man, woman, and child in Iceland. By the end of the same period, the cost of living index was 7.5 times higher than it had been in 1939, and wages paid for unskilled labor were 12 times higher than their prewar levels.

The demand for labor created by the Keflavík airport was responsible not only for providing full employment for Iceland's labor force, but also for causing distinct shortages of labor in the country's basic occupations of farming and fishing. The government sought to remedy this situation by a variety of measures, including subsidization of farm and fisheries production, utilization of child labor, particularly during the summer months, and the encouragement of the importation of foreign labor. By mid-1956 there were nearly 1200 foreigners employed in Iceland, of whom over half were Faeroese working in the fishing fleet; most of the remainder were Danes and West Germans employed in agriculture and the service occupations.

There seems little doubt but that the emergence of the Keflavík airport helped to hasten the transformation in Iceland's occupational structure which had been going on since about 1880. In the single decade from 1940 to 1950, the number of persons employed in industry surpassed the number engaged in each of the traditional livelihoods of farming and fishing. Thus, from its third-place position when the Americans arrived, manufacturing has jumped into first place among the occupations of Iceland. Likewise by 1950 there were more persons employed in the service occupations than in fishing, and the number of Icelanders earning their support from construction was almost equal to the number dependent on fishing. While these changes undoubtedly would have occurred in any event during the country's normal economic evolution, it seems clear that they scarcely would have occurred with such rapidity or vigor had it not been for the artificial stimulation provided by the large-scale American expenditures at Keflavík.

Concurrent with these changes in the country's occupational structure was a significant shift in the distribution of the island's inhabitants. A study of the population trends in Iceland reveals that the growth rate of the southwest, already high since 1900, took a further upswing after 1940. In all other regions of the country, however, the population either remained relatively stationary or actually declined in the same period. Virtually all of the increase in the southwest was recorded in existing towns and villages, though several new agglomerated settlements likewise came into being. Keflavík grew from a village of 1300 to a town (incorporated in 1949) numbering more than three times that figure today. The population of neighboring settlements swelled in almost direct proportion to their proximity to Keflavík. While the growth of Reykjavík and the spawning of suburbs around the Icelandic capital are distinct phenomena in their own right, it seems likely that the presence of the airport exerted at least a strong indirect influence in these instances as well.

The Americans' presence at Keflavík has left its most dynamic imprint on the material well-being and standard of living of the Icelanders. Within half a generation the last of the traditional sod houses has given way to modern concrete dwellings and the pack horse has been replaced by the automobile. In 1940 only one Icelander in 60 owned an automobile; today the ratio is one in nine. While no statistics are readily available, it is probable that the number of household appliances and other creature comforts has increased in a roughly similar proportion. Of greatest geographic significance, however, is the fact that the increase in material wealth has taken place very unevenly from region to region. This is effectively illustrated by the fact that the per capita ownership of automobiles in the southwest is approximately twice as great as that of some of the outlying districts of the north and east. It is also revealed by a comparison of data on per capita income by areas for two representative years. In 1951, a year when U.S. construction activity was *not* going on at Keflavík, the highest per capita income was found in Reykjavík, where the national average was exceeded by nearly 24 percent. In the same year, Keflavík had the lowest per capita income of any town in southwestern Iceland, although it too exceeded the national average by 11 percent. In 1953, when construction at the airport was it its peak following the base's reactivation, Keflavík supplanted Reykjavík as the wealthiest town in the country, recording in that year a per capita income 33 percent above the national average. The "spill-over" from Keflavík in 1953 also gave the surrounding rural district the distinction of being the only county in the country whose per capita income exceeded the national average. Though the outlying towns demonstrated no uniform pattern, in the rural districts the per capita income declined with increasing distance from the Southwestern Peninsula, yielding averages 30-40 percent below the national average over most of the north and east. While it is probable that the same general pattern of income distribution existed prior to the Americans' arrival, the emergence of the Keflavík airport served both to increase the regional disparities in wealth and to cause a significant shift of income to take place within the southwest itself.

But the American expenditures at Keflavík, large as they were, could not begin to pay for Iceland's phenomenal transformation from an almost medieval agrarian society to a modern urban-industrial nation. Many of the material gains which Iceland made after 1941 were accomplished at the expense of the country's balance of payments. In the prewar period it was an exceptional year when Iceland could not pay for all its imports with its exports of fish and still have a comfortable surplus left over. However, following her brusque introduction to the higher material culture of the Americans, Iceland underwent such a "revolution of expectations" that she became increasingly unable to catch and sell enough fish to pay for all the automobiles and appliances her people wanted. As a result, the gap between imports and exports tended to grow steadily wider, until in the mid-1950's it averaged some \$20-\$25 million each year.

From 1952 on, a shift in the pattern of Icelandic trade also began to manifest itself. In that year, motivated by the natural desire for a greater measure of economic security, Iceland unilaterally extended the limit of its territorial waters from three to four nautical miles. While the old three-mile limit followed the configuration of the coast, the new four-mile limit was measured from the headlands, thus closing off the many embayments which indent the island's shores. By this act she sought to restrict the activities of foreign fishermen along her coasts and thus help to insure the permanence of the fisheries on which she was so vitally dependent. The United Kingdom, which in some years had taken up to one-fourth of its total fish catch in Icelandic waters, was foremost among the countries which refused to recognize the new limits, and she retaliated by boycotting the landing of Icelandic fish at British ports. Britain had been Iceland's chief trading partner before World War II, when she was displaced by the United States, but even then she remained a strong second. With the outbreak of the fisheries dispute, however, commercial relations between the two countries began to deteriorate rapidly.

Such an open break between two NATO allies was much too tempting a prospect to go unnoticed by Moscow. The death of Stalin and Khrushchev's call for "peaceful coexistence" heralded the beginnings of an all-out trade offensive in which little Iceland promised to become one of the prime targets. Although the Soviet Union conducted almost no trade with Iceland in 1952, by 1955 it had become the leading buyer of Icelandic exports and the second largest supplier of Icelandic imports.

THE ELECTION OF 1956: NATO OR NOT?

By the spring of 1956 the economic and political cauldrons were boiling over in Iceland. The trade deficit was growing larger; inflation was running rampant; the labor shortage had pushed wage scales to the highest levels in Europe. There were social dislocations which the Icelanders likewise found increasingly unpleasant, such as the inevitable competition between Icelandic youths and American servicemen for the companionship of Icelandic girls. There was dismay among intellectuals who saw their proud, highly literate but woefully small culture being inundated by a tidal wave of "gum-chewing and comic-book-reading" Americans. And there were various religious groups who saw in all of these things the symptoms of moral and spiritual decay. Finally, late in March the Progressive party withdrew from the coalition government and joined with the opposition parties in voting to request the departure of the Americans from Keflavík. That the Althing's resolution embodied one of the primary objectives of Iceland's Communist minority was purely coincidental, for as the 31 to 18 vote showed, it had the support of many segments of the populace, each with their own pet reasons for favoring it.

The government in office, dominated by the pro-American Conservative party, could do nothing but call for new elections in order to let the Icelandic people at large express themselves on this critical issue. The Progressive party, which derived most of its support from the farmers, formed a coalition with the Labour party, whose strength came chiefly from the fishermen and workers in the towns. Thus, in those districts where the Agrarian element was strongest, the candidate ran on the Progressive ticket; where a more urban-industrial situation existed, the candidate was sponsored by the Labour party. Communist strength as usual was concentrated in the port towns of southwestern Iceland, chiefly, it would seem, amongst those segments of the populace who had benefited least from the presence of the Americans, such as fishermen and cannery workers. However, it should be pointed out that many intellectuals found their greatest identification with this party as well. (*Thjódviljinn,* the Communist party newspaper, is generally recognized as having some of the ablest journalists in the country on its staff and enjoys a circulation far beyond party membership circles.)

On Sunday, June 24, 1956, Icelanders flocked to the polls in an election that was to have widespread international as well as domestic repercussions. If the Americans were asked to leave, a key strategic base would have to be relinquished. How seriously would its loss cripple the NATO alliance? Might not its surrender pave the way for a Soviet take-over? At Keflavík itself, all construction activities had come to a halt following the Althing's original motion; until the issue was decided, everything would have to remain in a state of suspended animation.

When the returns were in, the pro-American Conservative party was seen to have scored the greatest gains in terms of the popular vote, picking up one additional representative from Reykjavík. However, three outlying seats in the north and east had been lost, for a net decline of two and a total of 19. The Progressives suffered more than a 6 percent decrease in popular vote, yet still managed to take one more parliamentary seat, giving them a total of 17. Their running mates in the Labor party increased both their popular vote and their parliamentary representation, winning two more seats for a total of 8. The Communists likewise scored an increase in the popular vote and annexed one additional seat for a total of 8. The tiny National Preservation party, which had appeared on the ballot for the first time in the previous election, now found most of its anti-American "fire" appropriated by the other larger parties, and was unable to win a single seat, losing the two it had gained in 1953.

The anti-American coalition of Progressives and Laborites thus emerged with 25 seats in the 52-member Althing, two short of an absolute majority. To be sure, they could count on the 8 Communist votes when the Keflavík issue was brought up for action. Indeed, with a mandate of nearly 58 percent of the popular vote, it was clear they they legally could move against the continuance of the base whenever they saw fit.

A new coalition cabinet (which included two Communist ministers) was formed at the end of July. One of the first moves of the new Foreign Minister was to fly to Norway to consult with his Norwegian counterpart, for the NATO countries had unanimously appealed to Iceland for continuance of the base. No communique was issued at the termination of his talks, and very shortly after returning from Norway the minister was "taken ill." The weeks dragged on, and still no decision was taken.

Obviously, the Progressive-Labor coalition was faced with a real dilemma. A responsible, popularly elected government had been given the mandate to request the American's withdrawal. Yet, what Icelandic government would be foolhardy enough to insist on shutting off the flow of dollars on which so much of the nation's economic life had come to depend? What government would have the courage to tell the Icelandic people that they had been living far above their means for over half a generation and that now it was time to face up to the necessity of accepting a lower standard of living? As it turned out, the paralysis of indecision was not broken by events in either Reykjavík or in Washington, but in Budapest. It was in the ruthless Soviet suppression of the Hungarian revolt that the Icelanders found a "justification" for withdrawing their request and permitting American forces to remain at Keflavík.

ECONOMIC STABILITY: AN ELUSIVE GOAL

Shortly thereafter, the fish-landing dispute with Great Britain was settled. This positive step was counterbalanced, however, by the fact that there had been no construction activities (hence, no payrolls!) at Keflavík for six to eight months, fishing had been poor, and the inflation was growing worse. Although a slight improvement was recorded in the country's balance of payments position, the excess of imports over exports in 1957 was still close to $24 million.

In January 1958 the Icelandic government received a proposal from Premier Bulganin of the Soviet Union that Iceland declare its neutrality. In its reply Iceland reiterated that its participation in NATO was purely defensive in character and that it would permit no missiles or nuclear weapons to be based on its territory. Indeed, waxing Icelandic enthusiasm for NATO was evidenced in the municipal elections held a few months later, when the Conservative party scored outsanding gains in all parts of the country.

However, on September 1, 1958, a new problem arose between Iceland and one of her NATO allies, the United Kingdom. On that date Iceland unilaterally extended her fisheries limit from 4 nautical miles to 12 nautical miles. Motivated by the same concern which prompted her action in 1952, Iceland found herself the target of a sharp British protest and a blatant refusal to respect the new limit. In fact, from September 1 on, British trawlers not only continued to fish within the 12-mile limit, but they were given a naval escort to protect them. Icelandic attempts to board and confiscate were met with ramming maneuvers, warning gunshots, and barrages of codfish. For her part in the "codfish war" Iceland had only the moral support of the Soviet Union, which once again took obvious delight in the internal strains within NATO that such a conflict produced.

Iceland's action in extending her fisheries limit was not a hasty or ill-considered move. On the contrary, ever since 1948 when she had first raised the issue in the United Nations General Assembly, she had been striving for international recognition of the need for revising the traditional but outmoded concept of the three-mile limit. In the United Nations Conference on the Law of the Sea held in Geneva during the spring of 1958, a majority of the nations voted in favor of the 12-mile limit, but not the required two-thirds. As a country which derives over 90 percent of her foreign exchange from fishing, Iceland assumed that most of the world would sympathize with her move even if they did not openly condone it. In effect, only the United Kingdom saw fit to challenge her. While trade between Iceland and Britain continued to decline, the overall balance of payments position improved somewhat, resulting in an excess of imports over exports for 1958 of just over $20 million.

Throughout 1958 the wage and price spiral continued, and ultimately its effects brought down the government. The biggest issues during the 1959 election were inflation and electoral reform, the latter necessitated by the increasing shift of population from rural to urban areas. Over the protests of the Progressive party, whose chief support came from the agrarian interests, the other three parties succeeded in pushing through the electoral reform. A second election in October, the first to be held under the new law, created a 60-member Althing with 5 to 14 members representing each of eight constituencies, all chosen on the basis of proportional representation. A new Conservative-Labor coalition cabinet was formed which immediately set about trying to halt the country's runaway inflation. By the end of 1959 the trade deficit was running at a rate of nearly $30 million a year.

Besides taking foreign loans to the full extent of the country's capacity to repay, the new government also instituted a drastic devaluation of the krona, the discontinuance of export subsidies, a reduction in investment, and an intensive program to cut credit and encourage savings. As a direct result of this "austerity" program, Iceland's balance of payments deficit for 1960 was brought down sharply to just over $19 million for the year. On the international scene, the opening of the United Nations Conference on Maritime Limits in Geneva in March prompted the British to withdraw their trawler fleet and its naval escorts just before the meeting got underway. This did not, however, present them from playing havoc with Icelandic nets as a parting gesture. Although the conference itself was a failure, the British adopted a more conciliatory attitude and refrained from dispatching naval vessels into the contested waters. After further negotiations, a settlement of the "codfish war" was reached early in 1961. In return for British recognition of the 12-mile limit and the new base lines on which it is drawn, Iceland agreed to permit British trawlers to operate in limited areas for certain months of the year for a period of three years.

With its major international disputes resolved, the Icelandic government could once again devote its full attention to the continuing problem of inflation. Strict enforcement of the regulations already in effect, together with a further devaluation of the krona, brought the balance of payments deficit in 1961 to under $3.5 million—the lowest level in well over a decade. Although the deficit rose slightly in 1962 (to just over $5 million), the general satisfaction of the Icelandic electorate was evidenced in their returning to office the Conservative-Labor coalition which had governed the country since 1959. Nevertheless, most Icelanders realized that their prosperity was a fragile compound of fortuitous fishing and disbursements from a "foreign" military base whose future was at best problematical. In the dawning age of intercontinental missiles, the strategic significance of Keflavík could hardly be expected to remain undiminished.

8 *Norden: Crossroads*
of Destiny

THE five Nordic states stand at one of the great crossroads of human history. Geographically they have come to occupy a highly strategic location amidst the three greatest concentrations of economic and political power in the world—the United States to the west, the Soviet Union to the east, and Europe to the south. Yet, they themselves are both economically and politically weak when viewed against a global backdrop; this their history has all too clearly demonstrated. Even Sweden, the strongest of the Nordic nations, can hardly be assigned the status of a third-ranking power today. Thus, if the evolution of these states holds any lesson at all, it is that political strength is predicated on economic viability and that this in turn is dependent upon a broad and diverse resource endowment.

Geopolitically, then, the crossroads which Norden occupies is an uncomfortable one. No small or weak state, or group of states, can feel secure when it finds itself caught between larger, more powerful political entities. This is a fact of life which the Nordic countries have had to adjust to, each in its own way and each in its own time. And it is a fact of life which is likely to remain unchanged as long as the center of global power lies in the Western world.

For their own survival, indeed for the survival of Western civilization itself, if not of all mankind, the states of Norden must seek the avoidance of a thermonuclear war. The spheres of influence of the atomic powers now overlap each other in Norden so that any shift in the balance of power within this region could easily set off a dangerous chain reaction in the Arctic arena as a whole. The

Nordic states can only hope that no Great Power will make a move which will have such an effect.

In this regard, there is perhaps less concern about the conduct of the first-order powers, the United States and the Soviet Union, than there is about that of such second-rank states as West Germany and France. It is no secret that Denmark and Norway, especially, were not happy about the United States' insistence on rearming West Germany and making that country the cornerstone of the European NATO alliance. And certainly the continued pronouncements of West German and American leaders regarding German unification are hardly more reassuring to them than they are to the Eastern bloc states. As countries which have long suffered from German economic and political domination, Denmark and Norway have no desire to see a militant Germany arise which cannot be held in check by the United States.

The countries of Norden likewise view with some concern the policy being pursued by France. De Gaulle's grand design for a French-dominated Europe is as disquieting in its way as is German talk about reunification. If the national interests of France are put ahead of those of the broader European community, then little more than a continuance of the age-old power struggle can be anticipated. Thus, independence of action on the part of either West Germany or France could upset the detente reached by the United States and the Soviet Union, thereby seriously jeopardizing the position of Norden.

However, even if neither West Germany nor France makes a move which would threaten the political balance, either of them is capable of upsetting the economic balance. De Gaulle's veto of British admission to the Common Market likewise held out Denmark and Norway, while at the same time giving pause to Sweden, Finland, and Iceland. The Scandinavian states and Finland are associated with EFTA, but none of them can afford to be permanently barred from membership in the EEC, for much of their trade is already with these countries. Association with the Common Market will present great opportunities for all of the Nordic states, though admittedly the price of membership may come high for certain sectors of their economies. Here again, however, the decisions are not theirs to make, and they must content themselves with whatever role De Gaulle (in particular) is willing to assign them.

Nevertheless, there are some very important functions which the Nordic states are fulfilling quite independently of any Great Power's pressure or control. One of the most important of these is as international arbiters. For example, the choice of a Norwegian, Trygve Lie, to become the first Secretary-General of the United Nations, and of a Swede, Dag Hammarskjöld, to serve as its second, were concrete demonstrations of world respect for the rationality and objectivity of Scandinavian statesmanship. In the same way, Scandinavian troops have been welcomed as peace-keepers in such trouble-spots as the Gaza Strip, Katanga, and Cyprus, largely because the countries concerned know that the Scandinavian states have no ambitions or designs of their own to further. Indeed, few countries enjoy so high a reputation or possess so vast a reservoir of confidence and good will as do the Nordic nations.

As we have seen, Norden has earned its reputation as "Europe's quiet corner" only within the last half century, and even that brief span of history has been punctuated by several wars. The emergence of Norden as a region dedicated to international harmony and the peaceful solution of disputes has essentially taken place since 1919, when the "Nordic Union" was established to further cultural cooperation among the five sister states. Although attempts at military alliances in the interwar years and even after World War II were unsuccessful, progress has been rapid in the economic and social fields, especially in the last decade. One of the major steps taken in economic cooperation occurred in 1946 when Denmark, Norway, and Sweden agreed to establish the Scandinavian Airlines System. Rather than create separate, competing, and financially weak national airlines, they decided that the SAS consortium could most efficiently conduct the domestic and international air traffic of all three countries. Since that time, other noteworthy advances have been made, including the abolition of passports for inter-Nordic travel, the free migration of labor, the reciprocal extension of social benefits to Nordic nationals resident in other Nordic countries, the standardization of academic degree requirements, the cooperative editing of school textbooks, and the coordination of research activities and cultural exchange programs. Since 1952 these efforts have taken on more formal guidance with the annual meetings of the "Nordic Council," an advisory and planning group composed of ranking government officials from all five countries.

Because the nations of Norden have evolved such advanced forms of economic and social democracy, and because they have achieved such high standards of living within the framework of so niggardly an environment, they have become objects of study and admiration among many of the world's underdeveloped lands. One of the most valuable lessons to be learned from the evolution of the Nordic states is that real progress and prosperity come only with peace, a lesson from which the Great Powers likewise would stand to gain. In fact, until such time as the Great Powers can learn to relax in each other's presence, Norden's position will continue to be uncomfortable. True, the pessimist may hold that this day will never come, for the disparities of economic, social, and political ideology which exist between the West and the East appear irreconcilable to him. But, fortunately, this would hardly seem to be the case, for the course of economic and social evolution is itself leading the Great Powers toward the ideological crossroad which is presently occupied by the Nordic countries. Not only is the "free enterprise" economy of the United States becoming more subject to governmental intervention and direction, but the "state capitalism" of the Soviet Union is also showing signs of making some concessions to private initiative. Similarly, while the American citizen is asked to give up some measure of his personal freedom for the social good, his Russian counterpart is gradually being accorded a greater amount of personal liberty wherever this is thought to be consistent with the security of the state. Thus, this "moving together," however slow, erratic, and unconscious it may be, can only approximate the situation currently exemplified by the nations of Norden. As the West becomes more socially conscious and the East becomes more democratic, the emergence of social democracy in the Scandinavian sense promises a new era of peace and progress for all mankind. Norden can provide a model for the world, a meeting-ground of ideologies, a crossroads of destiny.

Selected Bibliography

The Region as a Whole

1. Malmström, Vincent H. "Northern Europe," in *A Geography of Europe*, 2nd edition, edited by George W. Hoffman. New York: Ronald Press, 1961, pp. 190-261.
2. Mead, William R. *An Economic Geography of the Scandinavian States and Finland*. London: University of London Press, Ltd., 1958.
3. O'Dell, Andrew C. *The Scandinavian World*. London: Longmans, Green & Co., Ltd., 1957.
4. Sömme, Axel (editor). *The Geography of Norden*. Oslo: J. W. Cappelens Forlag, 1960.

Individual Countries

1. Andersson, Yngvar, *et al*. *Introduction to Sweden*. 2nd edition. Uppsala: Almqvist & Wiksell, 1951.
2. Danstrup, John. *A History of Denmark*. Copenhagen: Wivel, 1948.
3. Floyd, Calvin J. "Svalbard: Crossroads of the Arctic," *American-Scandinavian Review*, Summer 1962, pp. 153-160.
4. Floyd, Calvin J. "The Sound Dues," *American-Scandinavian Review*, Winter 1962, pp. 386-396.
5. Friis, Erik J. "Standing Guard in Greenland," *American-Scandinavian Review*, Autumn 1960, pp. 241-249.
6. Hall, Wendy. *Green Gold and Granite, A Background to Finland*. 2nd edition. London: Max Parrish, 1957.
7. Haupert, J. S. "The Impact of Geographic Location upon Sweden as a Baltic Power," *Journal of Geography*, Vol. 58 (January 1959), pp. 5-14.
8. Jakobsson, Max. *The Diplomacy of the Winter War: An Account of the Russo-Finnish Conflict, 1939-40*. Cambridge: Harvard University Press, 1961.

9. Jutikala, Eino. *A History of Finland.* New York: Praeger, 1962.

10. Lange, Halvard. "The Foreign Policy of Norway," *American-Scandinavian Review,* Spring 1964, pp. 15-23.

11. Malmström, Vincent H. *A Regional Geography of Iceland.* Washington: National Academy of Sciences-National Research Council, 1958. Publication 584.

12. Mead, William R. "Finnish Karelia: An International Borderland," *Geographical Journal* 118 (1952), pp. 40-57.

13. Mortensen, Sverre (editor). *The Norway Year Book.* 6th edition. Oslo: Johan Grundt Tanum, 1962.

14. Nuechterlein, Donald E. *Iceland, Reluctant Ally.* Ithaca: Cornell University Press, 1961.

15. Örvik, Nils. "Europe's Northern Cap and the Soviet Union," *Occasional Papers in International Affairs,* Number 6, September 1963 (Harvard University Center for International Affairs).

Index